S0-BBX-141

The
Vegetarian Touch

The Vegetarian Touch

Introduced by Gail Duff

ARCO PUBLISHING, INC.
New York

Editor: Julia Canning
Art editor: Mike Rose
Production: Richard Churchill
US Consultant: Jenni Fleetwood

Published 1985 by Arco Publishing, Inc.
215 Park Avenue South, New York, NY 10003

© Marshall Cavendish Limited 1985

Library of Congress Cataloging in Publication Data

Main entry under title:
The Vegetarian touch.
1. Vegetarian cookery. I. Arco Publishing.
TX837.V428 1985   641.5′636   84-28450
ISBN 0-668-06508-7
    0-668-06512-5 (pbk.)

Printed and bound in Hong Kong by
Dai Nippon Printing Company

Contents

Introduction

Vegetarian food has become delicious and exciting – no longer is it "food fit for cranks and extremists". In fact many households, whether they are accustomed to eating meals without meat or not, are now turning toward vegetarian-style menus with enthusiasm.

The ingredients that make up vegetarian meals are combinations of the old favorites, such as cheese and eggs, together with newly accepted foods, such as chickpeas, millet and exotic vegetables. The mixture has enabled us to experiment with new tastes and textures and has led us to be far less conservative in our cooking and eating habits. A new breed of cooks, both professional and in the home, has for the past few years been developing new recipes and experimenting with new cooking methods to produce a real vegetarian cuisine. No one who likes good food, whether they are vegetarian or not, could fail to enjoy the dishes and ideas in the following pages.

The main reason why many people are becoming vegetarian at the moment is one of health. A vegetarian diet contains fewer animal fats than a meat diet and very often includes more whole grain products and fresh fruits and vegetables, all of which provide fiber as well as other nutrients.

Another good reason for including vegetarian meals in your weekly diet is the fact that they are very economical. You are not buying expensive protein foods, such as meat or fish, but relying more on vegetables, pulses and small amounts of cheese or nuts. This will help the family budget and also allow you to splash out on extra special ingredients when you are entertaining.

The recipes in this book are suitable for vegetarians and non-vegetarians alike. If you are a vegetarian family, the recipes will go a long way to ensuring that you are eating the widest possible range of delicious and nutritious foods. If you are going to continue to eat meat, but wish to include more meat-free recipes in your menu plan for the week, they will help to add variety to your diet. If you have one vegetarian in the family or are having vegetarian friends for a meal, they can be an absolute life-saver.

The same rules for menu planning apply to vegetarian dishes as they do to mixed diet dishes. Simply make them as varied as possible. An extreme example of a badly planned menu is a cheese dip for a first course, a cheese based main course and cheesecake for dessert. Instead, start with a soup or something nutty, such as Spinach nut pasties (page 42). Follow this with a cheese based dish such as Cheese and chive soufflé or Swiss cheese fondue (both on page 61), and finish with Spiced pears (page 98) or Red currant sherbet (page 102).

If your main meal is based on pulses, a cheesy first course, such as Melted Mozzarella sandwiches (page 39) or Tomatoes with cheese filling (page 33), would be quite appropriate.

Besides being more appealing to the palate, well balanced meals will provide a wide range of nutrients – an important factor in a vegetarian diet.

Planning Menus

The recipes are grouped under practical chapter headings so that they can be easily selected to create menus both for family meals and entertaining.

Vegetarian Ingredients

Cheese
Cheese is an excellent source of protein, vitamins A and D and also of vitamin B12, which is lacking in plant protein foods such as nuts and pulses. Basically, there are two types of cheese available, hard cheese and soft cheese.

Hard cheeses include the types such as Cheddar, Cheshire, Edam, Gouda, Gruyère, Emmenthal and Parmesan. Most have a high fat content. Cheddar and Gruyère have around 34g per 100g and Edam and Gouda 22g and 26g respectively.

The problem for most strict vegetarians up until recently has been that hard cheeses are made by adding the animal product, rennet, to the milk in order to curdle it. Now, however, rennet-free cheeses are available from most health stores. These are made in such varieties as Cheddar and Cheshire. If you enjoy Italian cookery, an excellent substitute for Parmesan is a small, hard Swiss cheese, often made in a pyramid shape, called Geska.

The rules for buying and storing vegetarian cheeses are the same as for conventionally made hard cheeses. They may well be vacuum packed, in which case keep them in the refrigerator, still in the pack, until about an hour before needed. Open the pack and let the cheese breathe for a while at room temperature. Once opened, wrap the cheese in plastic wrap or foil and store it again in the refrigerator.

If you find vegetarian cheeses too mild for your taste, store them, still in their pack, for up to two weeks in the refrigerator – this will mature their flavor.

Soft cheeses, such as cream, curd and cottage cheeses, fromage blanc and Quark are made without rennet and are therefore suitable for strict vegetarians. Cream cheese has a high fat content; ideally it should be kept for special occasions or mixed with other types. Small curd cottage cheese is a medium-fat cheese with a stiff texture and tangy but creamy flavor. Cottage cheese, with its soft, lumpy texture, is the lowest in fats. It has a pleasant bland flavour, which mixes well with both sweet and savoury ingredients.

Two other cheeses, not always readily available, but worth looking out for, are Quark and Fromage blanc. Quark is a low-fat cheese, made by introducing a yogurt-type culture to the milk which gives it a light, fresh flavor. Fromage blanc has a rich, creamy flavor but a thin texture; it is a low- to medium-fat cheese.

All soft cheeses should be stored in the refrigerator and ideally eaten within three days of purchase. Use them for dips, spreads, pâtés and salads. Beat them with eggs to make quiche fillings or with sweet ingredients to make cheesecakes.

Yogurt

Yogurt makes a useful between meals snack. It can be spooned over cereals or fresh, dried or cooked fruits and used in both sweet and savory dishes.

Yogurt contains vitamins A and D, some B vitamins, calcium and small amounts of protein. If eaten regularly, it will help the body to manufacture its own B vitamins. It can also reduce excess acid in the stomach and can, again if eaten frequently, help to reduce hay fever.

There are many different types of yogurt on the market. The fruit-flavored ones contain added white sugar and very often coloring and preservative. If health is your concern, it is better to buy natural yogurt and flavor it yourself.

Natural yogurts can be made from skim or whole milk, so choose the one which suits you best. Whole milk varieties contain more fat. Some varieties have extra vitamins A and D added; others have been made by adding sugar to the milk. Those to be found in health food stores are very often made from whole milk and yogurt culture alone. Goat's milk and sheep's milk varieties are also available.

Milk

Milk should be regarded more as a nutritious food than as a drink, since it contains a wide range of nutrients. Vitamins A, D and some B vitamins are present, plus calcium and a small amount of protein.

Whole pasteurised milk is the milk that has been heated to around 16F to destroy bacteria. Some nutrients are also destroyed. Whole milk contains at least 3.25 per cent milkfat and at least 8.25 per cent protein, lactose and minerals. It has a clearly defined cream line.

Homogenised milk has been heat treated to break up the fat globules and distribute them throughout the milk. There is therefore no cream line. Homogenised milk can be frozen.

Fortified milk, as its name suggests, has been enriched with extra vitamins (usually A and D). It may also have added minerals and protein. Fortified milk may be whole or skim.

Low Sodium milk is a special diet product, available in liquid and powdered forms. Most of the sodium has been replaced by potassium.

Skim milk is pasteurised milk that has had virtually all its fat content removed. It is lower in vitamins A and D than whole milk. Semi-skimmed milk has had some of the fat removed, while skim dry milk solids powder is produced by spray-drying skimmed milk.

Goat's milk Goat's milk is becoming increasingly popular as it has been found that both children and adults who are allergic to cow's milk can drink goat's milk without problems. Goat's milk has a higher mineral content than cow's milk, slightly more vitamin A and twice the vitamin D. It has slightly more fat but this is distributed throughout the milk, making it more easily digestible. Goat's milk can be bought from some health stores and larger supermarkets.

Pasteurised milks will keep in a refrigerator for up to three days or in a cool larder for up to two.

Eggs

Eggs are another high protein food, providing an excellent source of vitamin B12. They also contain other B vitamins, vitamins A and D, small amounts of vitamin E and iron, calcium, potassium and magnesium. They are digested very slowly and therefore make meals that will keep you satisfied for a long time. Easy to eat and highly nutritious, they make an ideal food for all the family, from babies of eight months to grandparents.

Eggs are one of the most versatile foods in anyone's kitchen. They can be served at any time of the day and in both sweet and savory dishes. Try them boiled, scrambled or fried for snack meals, or turn them into omelets, soufflés, soufflé omelets or roulades.

Vegetables

Needless to say, vegetables play a large part in a vegetarian diet. In fact there are so many interesting varieties, supplying such a wide range of goodness, that they should be an important part in the daily menus of everyone. Turn them into soups or delectable appetizers. Make a crunchy vegetable salad as a light meal, or serve hot vegetables as an accompaniment to a main meal. You can even make a main dish with a vegetable base. See Bulgarian vegetable stew (page 45).

Much of our vitamin C comes from vegetables, mainly from the green, leafy types but also, surprisingly, from ingredients like potatoes and cauliflower. Carrots, other red colored vegetables and some of the darker green leaves provide vitamin A. The root vegetables, asparagus and beans provide B vitamins, while vitamin K is found in significant amounts in green vegetables.

Most vegetables are a good source of potassium and also supply plenty of fiber.

When buying vegetables always make sure that they look fresh. At home, keep them in a cool, dark place. Leafy greens and salad vegetables are best stored in a plastic bag in the bottom of the refrigerator. Mushrooms will keep well in a paper bag inside a plastic one. Leave root vegetables and onions unwashed or peeled, and store in a cool larder.

Fresh fruit

Fresh fruit can make a sweet, juicy snack at any time of the day. Serve it chopped into müsli or other cereals at breakfast; eat it with cheese for lunch; add it to vegetable soups and some savory dishes (see Curried apple soup page 14); and use it for all kinds of desserts from a fresh fruit salad to a Hazelnut and raspberry meringue (page 103).

Fresh fruits are an excellent source of dietary fiber, most contain good supplies of vitamin C. Some fruits will also provide vitamin A.

Always make sure that fruit really is fresh when you buy it. Store apples, pears and citrus fruits in a cool, dark place for up to one week. Soft fruits are best eaten on the day of purchase, but will keep in a cool place for up to a day. Refrigerating them tends to harm their flavor. Stone fruits will

keep in the refrigerator for up to two days, grapes and kiwi fruits for up to four days.

Dried fruit

In a healthy diet, dried fruits are excellent to use as alternative sweeteners. Cook cooking apples with chopped dates, for example, and there is no need to add sugar. Müslis and other breakfast cereals can also be sweetened entirely with dried fruits. The traditional use for dried fruits is in baking. See such recipes as Dundee cake and Apricot spice cake (both on page 110).

There is no vitamin C in dried fruits, but most are good sources of vitamin B1 and peaches and apricots of vitamin A. The mineral content is high and all are excellent sources of dietary fiber.

If you buy dried fruits from the supermarket you will notice that they look very shiny and do not stick together. This is because they have been coated with a mineral oil. Wash this off the fruits before using – put the fruits in a colander and rinse them with cold water. The varieties that you can usually buy in wholefood stores have no coating and therefore look duller and stickier.

Dried fruits keep well in airtight containers for up to one month. After this they may start to dry or form a sugary coating – they can still be used for cooking but are not so good raw.

Pulses

The term pulses covers the many varieties of dried beans, peas and lentils. These are invaluable in a vegetarian diet since they are excellent sources of protein, some B vitamins and iron. They must however be eaten with a grain product in order to supply your body with the right sort of protein. Beans on toast is the obvious example, but see also Moors and christians (page 57) and Soy burgers (page 54). The chick-pea dip known as Hummus (page 26), eaten with pita bread, is another perfect combination.

Pulses are now widely available in supermarkets and health food shops. Store them in airtight containers for up to 6 months. After this their skins may toughen causing the cooking time to be longer.

The method of cooking all the types of pulse is the same except for the timing. Recent research has shown that some types, in particular red, black, brown and white kidney beans, flageolets and pinto, navy and adzuki beans, may cause stomach upsets if they have not been boiled rapidly for at least 10 minutes, so incorporate this into your soaking and cooking method.

Beans can either be soaked overnight or quick-soaked on the same day. To soak overnight, simply leave them, covered with cold water, in a saucepan. When you are ready to cook them, first bring them to a boil, boil for 10 minutes and then drain. Cook them finally in fresh water. To quick-soak beans, put them into a saucepan and cover with cold water. Bring them to a boil and boil for 10 minutes. Off heat, let the beans soak for 2 hours. Drain and cook with fresh water.

Cooking times:
Mung beans, adzuki beans: 45 – 60 minutes
Black-eyed peas: 1 hour
Kidney beans, navy beans, flageolets: 1½ – 2 hours
Butter beans: 2 hours
Chick-peas: up to 3 hours
Soy beans: 4 hours

Whole lentils can be soaked in cold water for 1-2 hours before cooking. This speeds up the cooking time slightly but is not absolutely essential. They become soft in 45 minutes to 1 hour. Split red lentils and split yellow and green peas need no soaking. They are usually used for making soups or purées and will soften in 45 minutes.

Once pulses have been cooked, they become an extremely versatile ingredient in the vegetarian kitchen. They might seem a little bland when served completely plain, but add a tasty dressing and some chopped raw vegetables and they become an appetizing and colorful salad. See Two-bean salad (page 72). Add spicy vegetable sauces and you have delicious main meals. Spoon them on top of rice, layer them in a lasagne, put them into pasties and pies or purée them to make dips, pâtés and croquettes.

Pulses need not be completely cooked before adding them to other dishes, pro-

vided you observe the rules for initially boiling pulses such as kidney beans. They can actually be cooked with stock, vegetables and flavouring ingredients to make casseroles and soups. See Bean and vegetable soup (page 16) and Lentil and lemon soup (page 19).

The soy bean

The soy bean is so versatile that it deserves a special mention. It is high in protein and B vitamins, and has a delicious glossy texture when cooked. There are many soy bean products which are extremely useful in vegetarian cookery.

Soy sauce This is used widely in China and Japan and will add a salty flavor to soups, casseroles, salad dressings and stir-fried dishes.

Miso This is a thick, dark brown paste made from fermented soy beans. It is used in soups and vegetable casseroles to add protein, B vitamins and flavor.

Tofu This is also known as soy bean curd and is like a soy bean cheese. It comes in soft white blocks and has until now only been used in Eastern dishes. However, wholefood and vegetarian cooks have found that it is good in sauces, salad dressings and cheesecakes.

Soy flour This is a high protein flour made from finely ground soy beans. Small amounts can be added to baked goods and it can be used for sauces.

Soy milk This is a substitute milk made from soy beans. It looks and tastes very much like the real thing and can be used in the same way. It is ideal for those allergic to cow's milk.

Nuts and seeds

Nuts and seeds will also provide protein in a vegetarian diet but, like pulses, they must be combined with a grain product in order to supply the right type of protein for good health. The children's favorite – peanut butter on wholewheat bread – is a simple example. See also Nutty brown rice (page 56).

Nuts and seeds are also rich in minerals and contain, in varying quantities, B vitamins, and vitamins C, D and E. Never buy more than one month's supply of nuts or seeds at a time and store them in airtight containers.

Nuts are extremely versatile. Add them to müsli or cereals for breakfast, or nibble them with dried fruit. They also make nutritious main meals, such as Carrot and nut roast (page 55), or delicious desserts, like Date and walnut apples (page 98).

Of the seeds, sesame seeds feature strongly in vegetarian cookery, tahini, a paste made from ground sesame seeds, is handy for dips and dressings.

Cereals

There are many ingredients that come under the general heading of cereals, all of which add variety and goodness to the vegetarian diet. Both refined and unrefined cereals can be used, but the unrefined whole grains are the healthiest, providing more B vitamins, iron and calcium and a great deal more fiber. They are important in a vegetarian diet as they must be combined with pulses, nuts and seeds to make high protein meals.

Wheat Wholewheat grains can be cooked whole and served as an accompaniment to a main meal.

Cracked wheat can be soaked and used as a salad, but most often it is sprinkled over breads.

Bulgur (burghul) wheat has been pre-cooked and cracked. Before serving, it need only be soaked for a time in cold water. Use it for salads such as Bulgur wheat and parsley salad (page 68). It can also be used in casseroles.

The main use of wheat in the Western World is to grind it to make flour. Wholewheat flour is produced by simply grinding the grains, taking nothing away and adding nothing so that all the goodness and fiber are left.

Wholewheat, wholegrain or Graham flours have had some of the outercoating or bran removed, but the germ which contains most of the vitamins and minerals still remains. They are unrefined and unbleached.

White flour has had all the bran and most of the germ removed in order to make it easier to mill and to improve its keeping qualities, but leaving a product which has lost much of its goodness. Some B vitamins and iron must, by law, be added back artificially.

Unbleached white flour has not undergone a chemical bleaching process, leaving it creamy colored.

Bread flour is produced from what is known as hard wheat. It has a high gluten content and is an enriched flour.

Gluten flour is also milled from hard wheat. It is high in protein, low in calories and is used for making "slimming" breads.

Wheat germ is the tiny nutritious part of the wheat grain. It is high in B vitamins, iron and vitamin E and can be sprinkled over cereals and chopped fruit or added to bread mixes.

Wheat bran is the outer coating of the wheat grain and is high in fiber. Sprinkle it over cereals or use it as a coating for croquettes.

Semolina flour is hard wheat which has been coarsely ground. Use it for milk puddings.

Pasta is also made from a hard wheat flour. Both white and wholewheat varieties are available in a wide variety of shapes and sizes. Spinach pasta can also be bought in the form of tagliatelle or lasagne. Fresh pasta is available from delicatessens which specialize in Italian food. Pasta makes a wide range of substantial main meals. See Creamy rigatoni (page 65) and Lentil lasagne (page 64).

Oats Oats can be bought in the form of whole oat grains (sometimes called groats) which can be cooked in a similar way to rice; coarse oatmeal which is normally used for porridge; and medium and fine oatmeal which are used for baked goods. Oat Flakes are used mainly for müsli and also make delicious flapjacks and crumble toppings. Porridge oats have been steamed so that they cook quickly to make a creamy breakfast.

Barley Pearl barley and whole barley grains are used to enrich soups and casseroles (see Leek and barley soup page 18). Barley flakes are similar to rolled oats and are sometimes added to müsli; while barley flour can be used to make light pastries.

Rye Rye is most often sold in the form of flour, which is used with whole wheat flour to make rye bread. Coarse ground rye is sold as rye meal.

Rice Both white and brown rice can be used in vegetarian cookery, but brown rice is the most nutritious since, like wholewheat, it still has its outer coating of bran. It also contains more iron, calcium, protein and B vitamins than the white varieties. Both long and short grain varieties of brown rice are available. The long grain is used mainly in savory dishes, such as pilaffs, and is also cooked plainly to be served as an accompaniment. Short grain brown rice can be used for risottos as well as for rich milk puddings.

Brown rice takes longer to cook than white, 40-45 minutes as opposed to 15-20 minutes.

Buckwheat The tiny, heart-shaped grains of buckwheat are most often cooked to make a grain side dish known as Kasha. They have a distinct nutty flavour. Buckwheat flour can be made into pancakes and muffins. It is also made into a quick-cooking pasta.

Millet Takes the form of round, tiny yellow grains which, when cooked, make a fluffy, light textured side dish.

Sweeteners

A vegetarian diet need not be an austere one. You can still enjoy desserts and candies. There are many different types of sweetener available, some are slightly healthier than others.

Sugar White sugar is made up only of sucrose which provides calories but no other nutrients. Brown sugar contains small traces of minerals. Dark brown sugar contains small amounts of minerals and enough B vitamins to ensure its digestion without depleting your body's supplies. Turbinado sugar, which is a partially refined sugar, is dark and rich, and is a better source of minerals and also contains B vitamins.

Molasses is high in minerals and B vitamins. It can be used in baking and is good for flavoring and sweetening cooked fruit.

Honey contains small amounts of vitamins A and C and those of the B group. The energy it gives is quickly available to the body and lasts longer than that obtained from white sugar. Honey has two thirds the calories of sugar, and is much sweeter, so that you need less.

Maple syrup is derived by boiling and reducing the sap of North American maple trees. It contains a high proportion of sugars but is also rich in minerals.

Malt extract is made from germinated barley grains. It is digested more slowly than sucrose so gives a constant supply of energy rather than a quick lift. It contains small amounts of protein, B vitamins and minerals.

Fats and oils

Butter is the first choice for many vegetarians, though others prefer to use vegetable oils or a soft vegetable margarine, all of which are high in polyunsaturated fats and low in cholesterol.

When buying margarine, read the labels and choose one that is made only from vegetable ingredients. The softer a margarine, the more polyunsaturated fats it contains. Vegetable margarine can be spread on bread and used in baking. You can sauté with it and toss it into cooked vegetables.

The best oils to buy are the named oils such as olive, sunflower, safflower, soy, peanut, corn and sesame. Olive oil is the best for salads. Sunflower is a good universal oil, which can be used for both salads and for sautéeing. Peanut oil is the one frequently chosen by the Chinese for stir-frying. Corn oil can be used for deep frying or for making cakes and pastries.

Savory flavorings

Herbs and spices These feature frequently in vegetarian cooking and can turn plain ingredients into exotic dishes with flavors from all over the world.

Many recipes specify only the amount of fresh herbs. If you only have dried, use one third of the quantity of fresh herbs given. Dried herbs are not suitable for uncooked recipes such as dips, but they can be added to salads if they are soaked in the dressing for 30 minutes beforehand.

Many supermarkets now stock a wide range of fresh herbs. You can also try growing your own.

Store dried herbs in airtight containers and keep them for no longer than a year. Spices should also be bought in small amounts, kept in airtight containers and, like herbs, stored for no longer than a year, after which their flavor may deteriorate or alter.

Yeast extract A yeast extract, such as Brewer's yeast, will give extra flavor to savory vegetarian dishes, particularly nut roasts, patties and vegetable casseroles.

Sweet flavorings

Vanilla and almond extracts Natural vanilla and almond extracts can be bought from delicatessens and health food stores. They have a finer flavor than those labelled 'flavoring'. Use them in desserts and in baking.

Carob Carob powder is a popular substitute for cocoa powder. It is produced from the carob bean and is high in vitamins and minerals. It is far sweeter than cocoa, so dishes made with it need less sugar. It is caffeine-free.

Setting agents

Whether making savory molds or sweet "gelatins" and mousses, some setting agent has to be used. Non-vegetarians can use gelatine, but as this is an animal product strict vegetarians prefer to use a substitute.

Agar-agar is a freeze-dried seaweed which comes in the form of small, off-white flakes. Two to three teaspoons should set 600ml/1 pint liquid. In order to achieve a set, boil the flakes in all or some of the cold liquid, according to individual recipes.

Soups

*Soups add variety and interest to vegetarian meals –
start a meal in style with a smooth, chilled soup or warm
the family with a nourishing meal-in-a-bowl.*

Vegetable stock

MAKES ABOUT 5 PINTS

1 large onion, finely chopped

3 large carrots, chopped

3 celery stalks with leaves left on, roughly chopped

1 large turnip or parsnip, roughly chopped

1/4 cup margarine

1 teaspoon light brown sugar

5 pints hot water

1 large bouquet garni, consisting of 8 parsley sprigs, 2 thyme sprays and 2 bay leaves, tied together

6 white peppercorns

1 1/2 teaspoons salt

2 whole cloves

1 Melt the margarine in a large saucepan over moderate heat. Add the onion, carrots, celery, turnip and sugar and cook, stirring frequently, for 8-10 minutes until the onion is soft and golden brown.

2 Pour in the hot water, then add the bouquet garni, white peppercorns, salt and cloves. Bring the liquid to a boil, stirring frequently, then lower the heat and simmer, stirring occasionally, for 45 minutes.

3 Off heat, pour the vegetables and liquid through a fine wire strainer into a large mixing bowl. Using the back of a wooden spoon, press firmly down on the vegetables to extract all the juices. Discard the contents of the strainer.

4 Set the vegetable stock aside until completely cool.

5 Transfer to a container, cover with plastic wrap and store for 2-3 days in the refrigerator, or use this homemade vegetable stock as required.

Summer pea soup

SERVES 4

3 lb fresh peas in the pod

2 tablespoons butter

1/2 Bermuda onion, minced

4 outer leaves romaine lettuce, shredded

2 1/2 cups hot vegetable stock

salt and freshly ground black pepper

2/3 cup plain yogurt

1/2 teaspoon lemon juice (optional)

1 Hull the peas and weigh out about 18 oz. Reserve 3-4 of the best empty pea pods.

2 Melt the butter in a large, heavy-bottomed saucepan over low heat. Add the onion, lettuce and the reserved pea pods, cover the pan and cook the vegetables gently for 10 minutes, stirring occasionally.

3 Add the peas to the pan, pour in the hot stock and season to taste with salt and pepper. Bring slowly to a boil, cover, lower heat and simmer until the peas are very tender.

4 Remove the saucepan from the heat, discard the pods, and let the soup cool slightly. Purée the soup in a blender, a batch at a time. Reserve 4 teaspoons yogurt and add the rest to the final batch of purée and blend this batch again.

5 Pour all the puréed soup into a bowl and refrigerate for about 2 hours, stirring occasionally.

6 Just before serving, taste and adjust the seasoning; sharpen the soup with a few drops of lemon juice if liked. Pour the soup into 4 individual bowls and swirl 1 teaspoon plain yogurt into each. Serve at once.

Gazpacho

SERVES 4

1 lb tomatoes, peeled and chopped

1/2 cucumber, pared and chopped

1 green pepper, seeded and chopped

1 small onion, roughly chopped

1 clove garlic, chopped

2 slices white bread, crusts removed and crumbed

1 teaspoon salt, or to taste

2 tablespoons red wine vinegar

1 quart ice water

1/3 cup olive oil

To serve

bread cubes, sautéed until golden

chopped hard-cooked egg

finely chopped cucumber

finely chopped green pepper

finely diced onion

1 In a large bowl, combine the tomatoes, cucumber, green pepper, onion, garlic, bread, salt and vinegar. Add the water and mix thoroughly. Purée the mixture in a food processor or blender until smooth. Return the purée to the large bowl and beat in the olive oil in a thin, steady stream. Cover the bowl with plastic wrap and refrigerate for about 2 hours until thoroughly chilled.

2 When the soup is well chilled, stir thoroughly and taste and adjust seasoning. Pour into 4 chilled individual soup bowls and pass the sautéed bread cubes, chopped egg, cucumber, green pepper and diced onion separately.

Gazpacho, a classic Spanish soup

SERVES 4

2½ cups thinly sliced carrots
1 tablespoon vegetable oil
1 onion, finely chopped
2 tablespoons medium-dry sherry
2½ cups vegetable stock
salt and freshly ground black pepper
grated rind of 1 orange
juice of 3 large oranges
For garnish
4 very thin orange slices, rinds removed
1 small carrot, shredded

1 Heat the oil in a saucepan, add the onion and sauté gently for 5 minutes until soft and lightly colored. Add the sherry and bring to a boil.
2 Add the sliced carrots and stock to the pan and season to taste.
3 Bring to a boil, stirring, then lower the heat, cover and simmer gently for 45 minutes until the carrots are very tender. Let cool.
4 Pass the soup through a strainer or purée in a blender. Pour the soup into a bowl, cover and refrigerate for at least 2 hours or overnight.
5 Just before serving, stir the orange rind and juice into the soup, then taste and adjust seasoning. Pour into 4 chilled individual soup bowls, float 1 orange slice on top of each bowl and arrange a little shredded carrot on top of the slices. Serve at once.

Chilled cucumber soup

SERVES 4

1 large unpared cucumber, finely shredded
1 pint plain yogurt
2 tablespoons wine vinegar
2 tablespoons chopped fresh mint
2 tablespoons seedless raisins
2 hard-cooked eggs, finely chopped
1 large clove garlic, minced
1 teaspoon superfine sugar
1 large crisp eating apple, cored and chopped
⅔ cup sour cream

Curried apple soup

SERVES 4

1 lb eating apples
few drops of lemon juice
1 tablespoon butter
½ Bermuda onion, finely chopped
1 tablespoon mild curry powder
2½ cups hot vegetable stock
piece of cinnamon stick
⅔ cup milk
⅓ cup light cream
thin lemon slices and watercress sprigs, for garnish

1 Pare, core and chop the apples, placing them in a bowl of cold water mixed with the lemon juice, to prevent discoloration.
2 Melt the butter in a heavy-bottomed saucepan. Thoroughly drain the apples and add them to the pan with the onion. Cover and cook gently, stirring occasionally, until apples and onion are soft but not colored.
3 Add the curry powder and cook over moderate heat, stirring, for 2-3 minutes. Pour in the hot stock and add the cinnamon stick. Bring to a boil, cover the pan, lower the heat and simmer for 10 minutes, stirring. Remove the cinnamon.
4 Purée the soup in a blender or pass through a strainer. Let cool, then stir in the milk and cream. Refrigerate, covered, for 2 hours.
5 Stir the soup and pour into 4 individual bowls. Garnish and serve.

1 In a large bowl combine all the ingredients and stir well to mix them thoroughly.
2 Cover the bowl and refrigerate for at least 3 hours.
3 Pour the soup into a tureen or spoon straight into individual bowls and serve chilled.

Yogurt and lemon soup

SERVES 6

2 1/2 cups plain yogurt, chilled
2 1/2 cups tomato juice, chilled
1 teaspoon tomato paste
1/2 small cucumber, pared and finely diced
1 green pepper, seeded and finely chopped
2 scallions, thinly sliced
juice and grated rind of 1 large lemon
salt and freshly ground black pepper
large pinch of cayenne
1/2 teaspoon mild paprika
1 tablespoon chopped chives
thin lemon slices and slivered almonds, for garnish

1 Tip the yogurt into a large bowl and gradually beat in the tomato juice and paste until the mixture is smooth and well blended.
2 Stir in the cucumber, green pepper, scallions, lemon juice and rind. Season with salt and black pepper and stir in the cayenne and paprika.
3 Cover and refrigerate until needed. Just before serving, stir in the chopped chives. Pour into individual bowls, garnish and serve.

Chilled fruit soup

SERVES 4

1/2 pint fresh or frozen red currants
1/2 pint fresh or frozen black currants
3/4 pint fresh or frozen raspberries
3 3/4 cups water
3 tablespoons tapioca or sago
2 inch cinnamon stick
2 thinly pared strips lemon rind
1 cup sugar
6 tablespoons sour cream

Left: Curried apple soup is an exciting combination of flavors
Above: Chilled carrot and orange soup makes a popular appetizer

1 To prepare fresh fruit: Strip the currants from their stems by drawing a fork down each stem. Pick over the raspberries, and reserve 4 for the garnish.
2 Put the fruits in a large, heavy-bottomed saucepan with the water, tapioca, cinnamon stick, lemon rind and sugar.
3 Set the pan over moderate heat and bring to a boil. Lower the heat and cook the mixture gently, uncovered, for 20 minutes.
4 Off heat, discard the cinnamon stick and lemon rind. Pass the soup through a strainer. Cool, then refrigerate for 1 1/2 hours.
5 Pour the chilled soup into 4 chilled individual bowls. Beat the sour cream until smooth, then swirl a portion over each serving. Top each swirl of sour cream with a raspberry and serve at once.

Bean and vegetable soup

SERVES 4

1⅓ cups dried navy beans, soaked overnight and drained

1 tablespoon vegetable oil

1 large onion, chopped

2 leeks, chopped

3 celery stalks, chopped

2 carrots, sliced

2 cloves garlic, minced

3 cups vegetable stock

1 can (8 oz) tomatoes

1 teaspoon dried oregano

salt and freshly ground black pepper

1 Cover the beans with fresh hot water and boil for 10 minutes, then cover, lower the heat and simmer for about 2 hours until they are tender. Drain.
2 Heat the oil in a large saucepan, add onion and sauté for 2 minutes. Add leeks, celery, carrots and garlic to pan and cook for 2 minutes more.
3 Add the stock and beans, together with the tomatoes and their juice, the oregano and plenty of salt and pepper. Bring to a boil, then lower the heat, cover and simmer for 30 minutes until the vegetables are tender. Serve.

Leekie oat broth

SERVES 4

1 cup thinly sliced leeks

2½ cups vegetable stock or water

⅔ cup finely chopped carrots

½ teaspoon dried mixed herbs

salt and freshly ground black pepper

¼ cup porridge oats

⅔ cup milk

2 tablespoons light cream or evaporated milk

Above: Leekie oat broth, a thick hearty soup for winter days
Right: Chunky soy vegetable soup is a meal in itself

To serve

¼ lb Edam cheese, cubed

1 Pour the stock into a saucepan and bring to a boil. Add the leeks, carrots, herbs and salt and pepper to taste. Lower the heat, cover pan and simmer for 15 minutes or until the vegetables are tender.
2 Sprinkle the oats into the soup, stir in the milk and cook broth gently, uncovered, for 5 minutes, stirring occasionally, until thick. Stir in the cream and heat through gently.
3 To serve: Ladle into a warmed tureen or individual soup bowls and mix the cubes of Edam cheese into the soup. Serve at once, before the cheese has completely melted.

Finnish vegetable soup

SERVES 4-6

1 lb potatoes (preferably new), diced

3 medium carrots, diced

1 cup cauliflower flowerets

1/3 cup frozen peas

1/2 package (10 oz size) frozen sliced green beans

1 quart water

salt and freshly ground black pepper

2 tablespoons butter or margarine

1/4 cup all-purpose flour

1 large egg yolk

1/4 cup heavy cream

1/4 teaspoon mild paprika

To serve

2 tablespoons finely chopped fresh parsley

1/2 cup shredded sharp Cheddar or Cheshire cheese

1 Put the potatoes, carrots, cauliflower, peas, beans and water into a large saucepan. Season well with salt and pepper, bring to a boil, lower the heat and simmer uncovered for 10 minutes or until the potatoes and carrots are fork-tender.

2 Off heat, strain the vegetable stock into a large bowl. Reserve the cooked vegetables.

3 Melt the butter gently in the rinsed-out pan and sprinkle in the flour. Stir over low heat for 1-2 minutes until straw-colored. Off heat, gradually stir in the stock. Return to the heat and simmer, stirring, until thick and smooth.

4 In a small bowl, beat the egg yolk into the cream with the paprika. Gradually beat 1/4 cup of the hot thickened stock into the egg and cream, then slowly stir the mixture back into the remaining thickened stock in the pan. Return the reserved vegetables to the pan, taste and adjust seasoning and heat through. Do not boil or it may curdle. Add a little extra vegetable stock if the soup is too thick.

5 To serve: Ladle into 4 warmed individual soup bowls and sprinkle each serving with chopped parsley. Serve at once with shredded cheese passed separately.

Chunky soy vegetable soup

SERVES 4

2/3 cup soy beans, soaked in cold water overnight

1 tablespoon vegetable oil

1 large onion, sliced

2 leeks, thickly sliced

1/3 cup thickly sliced carrots

2 celery stalks, thickly sliced

1/3 cup cubed turnips

1 quart vegetable stock or water

1 tablespoon lemon juice

2 tablespoons tomato paste

1-2 tablespoons finely chopped mixed fresh herbs

1 cup thickly sliced zucchini

a few tender cabbage or spinach leaves, finely shredded or chopped

salt and freshly ground black pepper

2 teaspoons toasted sesame seeds, for garnish (optional)

1 Drain the soaked beans, then put into a saucepan and cover with fresh cold water. Bring to a boil and boil for 10 minutes, then lower the heat, cover and simmer for 1 1/2 hours.

2 After the beans have been cooking for 1 hour 20 minutes, heat the oil in a separate large saucepan. Add onion and sauté gently for 3 minutes until soft but not colored. Add the leeks, carrots, celery and turnips and cook, stirring, for a further 2 minutes.

3 Stir in the stock, lemon juice, tomato paste and herbs.

4 Drain the beans and add to the pan. Bring to a boil, then lower the heat slightly, cover the pan and simmer for 1 hour.

5 Add the zucchini and cabbage and continue to cook for a further 15 minutes or until the vegetables are tender. Season to taste.

6 Pour into warmed individual soup bowls and garnish with a sprinkling of sesame seeds, if liked. Serve at once.

Provençal vegetable soup

SERVES 4-6

1 large potato, diced

1 large onion, chopped

1 celery stalk, finely sliced

2 carrots, sliced

1 cup sliced green beans

1 cup sliced English runner beans or snake beans

2 zucchini, thickly sliced

7½ cups water

1 teaspoon salt

bouquet garni

1 cup dried wholewheat pasta shells or macaroni

Pistou sauce

3-4 large cloves garlic, peeled

4 tablespoons chopped fresh basil leaves

salt and freshly ground black pepper

½ cup grated Parmesan cheese

2 tomatoes, peeled, seeded and chopped

¼ cup olive oil

1 Put the water in a large Dutch oven, add the salt and bring to a boil. Add the bouquet garni, potato, onion, celery, and carrots. Bring back to a boil, then cover the pot, lower the heat and simmer for about 10 minutes until the vegetables are almost tender.

2 Add the beans, zucchini and pasta to the pot and simmer, uncovered, for 10-15 minutes until tender.

3 Meanwhile, make the pistou: Put the garlic in a mortar with the basil and salt and pepper to taste, then pound to a paste. Gradually work in the cheese, alternating with the tomatoes. Slowly work in the olive oil, a few drops at a time to start with, to make a thick sauce.

4 Remove and discard the bouquet garni from the soup. Blend ¼ cup of the hot soup into the sauce, then stir the mixture into the soup.

5 Taste and adjust the seasoning. Pour the Provençal vegetable soup into warmed individual soup bowls and serve at once.

Leek and barley soup

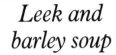

SERVES 4

4 leeks, sliced

⅓ cup pearl barley

1 tablespoon vegetable oil

1 small onion, chopped

2 carrots, sliced

1 can (16 oz) tomatoes

2½ cups vegetable stock or water

½ teaspoon dried mixed herbs

1 bay leaf

salt and freshly ground black pepper

1 can (about 8 oz) cannellini beans, drained

Cheesy bread

4 round slices French bread, ¾ inch thick

3 tablespoons butter, for frying

1 clove garlic, cut in half

1 cup shredded Cheddar cheese

1 Heat the oil in a large saucepan, add the onion, leeks and carrots and sauté gently for 3-4 minutes.

2 Add the tomatoes with their juice, the stock and the barley, herbs and bay leaf. Season to taste with salt and pepper. Bring to a boil, stirring, then lower the heat, cover and simmer for 50 minutes. Stir occasionally during this time.

3 Meanwhile, make the cheesy bread: Melt the butter in a skillet and when it sizzles add the slices of French bread. Cook over fairly high heat, turning once, until the bread is crisp and golden brown on both sides. Remove the fried bread from the pan, drain on absorbent kitchen paper and let cool.

4 Rub each side of fried bread with the cut sides of the garlic. Press the shredded cheese evenly onto the slices of bread, dividing it equally among them. Preheat the broiler to high.

5 Remove the bay leaf from the soup, stir in the drained beans and heat through. Taste and adjust the seasoning if necessary.

6 Broil the cheese-topped slices of bread until the cheese starts to bubble.

7 Ladle the soup into 4 warmed individual soup bowls and top each one with a slice of cheesy bread. Serve at once.

Thick country soup

SERVES 4

1 tablespoon vegetable oil

1 tablespoon butter

1 onion, chopped

1⅓ cups sliced carrots

1 package (about 4 oz) soup mix, containing a mixture of pulses with oatmeal as the thickener

1 quart vegetable stock

1 leek, white part only, chopped

1 celery stalk, chopped

1 teaspoon dried thyme

1 bay leaf

salt and freshly ground black pepper

1 tablespoon chopped fresh parsley

1 In a saucepan, heat the oil and butter and gently cook the onion and carrots for 10 minutes.

2 Add the soup mix together with the vegetable stock, leek, celery and herbs. Bring to a boil, then lower the heat, cover and simmer for about 45 minutes. Remove the bay leaf from the soup, if liked.

3 Season the soup to taste with salt and pepper and stir in the parsley.

4 Pour the thick country soup into a warmed soup tureen or divide among 4 individual bowls and serve at once, piping hot.

Lentil and lemon soup

SERVES 4

½ cup split red lentils, packed

1 tablespoon vegetable oil

2 celery stalks, chopped

1 medium onion, finely chopped

1 quart boiling water

4 vegetable bouillon cubes

grated rind and juice of 1 lemon

¼ teaspoon ground cumin (optional)

salt and freshly ground black pepper

1 red pepper, seeded and thinly sliced in rings

For garnish

1 lemon, thinly sliced

chopped chives (optional)

1 Melt the vegetable oil in a saucepan, add the celery and onion, then cover and cook gently for 4 minutes.

2 Remove the pan from the heat, then stir in the lentils and water, with the bouillon cubes. Add the lemon rind and juice, and the cumin, if using. Season to taste with salt and pepper. Cover and simmer over very gentle heat for 30 minutes.

3 Add the sliced pepper to the pan, cover and cook for a further 30 minutes. Taste and adjust seasoning.

4 Pour the soup into warmed serving bowls, float the lemon slices on top, then sprinkle over the chives, if using. Serve at once.

Left: Leek and barley soup has a scrumptious toast garnish
Below: Thick country soup makes a nourishing family supper dish

Left: *Mixed vegetable borscht*
Right: *Spinach and potato soup*

the rinsed-out pan and stir in the milk.
4 Heat the purée gently until simmering then remove from heat and stir in the shredded cheese. Season to taste with salt and pepper.
5 Pour the soup into 4 warmed individual soup bowls and swirl 1 tablespoon cream into each. Place a fourth of the cheese on top of each serving and sprinkle over a little chopped parsley. Serve at once.

Creamy spinach and potato soup

SERVES 4

1 lb spinach, central ribs removed, or 1
   package (10 oz) frozen spinach
1 lb potatoes, cut in chunks
2 tablespoons butter or margarine
1 onion, chopped
2½ cups vegetable stock
few sprigs of parsley
pinch of freshly grated nutmeg
⅔ cup milk
⅔ cup light cream
2 teaspoons lemon juice
salt and freshly ground black pepper
Cheese floats
4 slices French bread, cut diagonally in ¾
   inch thick slices
3 oz Cheddar cheese, thinly sliced

1 Melt the butter in a saucepan, add the onion and sauté over moderate heat for 3 minutes, stirring. Add the spinach, potatoes, vegetable stock, parsley and nutmeg.
2 Bring to a boil, then lower the heat, cover and simmer for about 20 minutes, until potatoes are tender.
3 Preheat the broiler to high.
4 Let the mixture cool slightly, then work in batches in a blender. Return to the rinsed-out pan, then stir in the milk, cream and lemon juice. Season with salt and pepper. Reheat very gently without boiling.
5 Meanwhile, make the cheese floats: Toast the slices of bread on one side, then lay the cheese slices on the untoasted sides and broil until the cheese has melted.
6 Pour the soup into 4 warmed individual bowls and top each with a cheese float. Serve at once.

Mixed vegetable borscht

SERVES 6

1 lb cooked beet, peeled
1 large onion
½ lb carrots
½ lb celery
5½ cups vegetable stock
1 tablespoon light brown sugar
2 tablespoons red wine vinegar
1 clove garlic, minced with a pinch of salt
freshly ground black pepper
For garnish
⅔ cup sour cream
1½ cups cooked and finely diced potato
2 tablespoons chopped fresh parsley

1 Cut all the vegetables in matchstick strips.
2 Bring the stock to a boil, add the vegetables, sugar, vinegar and garlic and season with the pepper. Cover, lower the heat and simmer for 20 minutes.
3 To serve, ladle soup into warmed individual bowls. Top each with a portion of sour cream. Scatter the diced potato on top and sprinkle over a little chopped parsley. Serve the vegetable borscht at once.

Cauliflower cheese soup

SERVES 4

2 cups small cauliflower flowerets
¼ cup butter
1 onion, chopped
1 potato, thinly sliced
1¼ cups vegetable stock
1¼ cups milk
½ cup shredded Cheddar cheese
salt and freshly ground black pepper
For garnish
¼ cup light cream
¼ cup shredded Cheddar cheese
1 tablespoon chopped fresh parsley

1 Melt the butter in a large saucepan, add the onion and sauté gently for 5 minutes until soft and lightly colored. Add the cauliflower flowerets and potato slices. Cover and cook the vegetables for 10 minutes.
2 Stir in the stock, bring to a boil, then cover, reduce heat and simmer for about 25-30 minutes, until all the vegetables are soft. Allow to cool slightly.
3 Transfer the vegetables and stock to the goblet of a blender and work until smooth. Off heat, return purée to

Creamy mushroom soup

SERVES 4

2¼ cups button mushrooms
¼ cup butter
2 tablespoons all-purpose flour
2½ cups milk
1 package (3 oz) cream cheese with chives
2 teaspoons lemon juice
salt and freshly ground black pepper
1 tablespoon chopped chives, for garnish

1 Finely chop the mushrooms, reserving 2-3 whole ones for the garnish. Melt half the butter in a skillet. Add the chopped mushrooms and sauté gently for about 5 minutes until soft. Set aside.

2 Melt the remaining butter in a large saucepan, sprinkle in flour and stir over low heat for 1-2 minutes until it is straw-colored. Remove from the heat and gradually stir in milk. Return to the heat and simmer, stirring, until the mixture is thick and smooth.

3 Remove from the heat, add the cheese a little at a time and stir until melted. Stir in the mushrooms, their juices and the lemon juice. Season to taste with salt and pepper. Return the pan to the heat and simmer for 2-3 minutes.

4 Pour into 4 warmed soup bowls. Float a few slices of mushroom on top of each serving. Sprinkle lightly with chives and serve at once.

Green pepper cream soup

SERVES 4

½ lb green peppers, seeded
2 tablespoons butter or margarine
1 large onion, chopped
1 clove garlic, chopped
2 tablespoons all-purpose flour
2½ cups vegetable stock
1 teaspoon chopped fresh herbs or ½ teaspoon dried mixed herbs
salt and freshly ground black pepper
1 teaspoon lemon juice
⅔ cup light cream

1 Cut a few very thin rings from one of the peppers and set aside for the garnish. Chop the remainder.

2 Melt the butter in a heavy-bottomed saucepan. Add the chopped peppers, onion and garlic and cook over very low heat for about 10 minutes, stirring frequently, until the vegetables are soft but not brown.

3 Sprinkle in the flour and cook for 1-2 minutes, stirring, then gradually stir in the stock. Add the herbs, and season to taste with salt and pepper. Cover and cook gently for 20-25 minutes until the vegetables are tender.

4 Let cool slightly, then transfer to a blender and blend for about 5 seconds until smooth. If you do not have a blender, work the vegetables through a strainer while still hot. Return the soup to the rinsed-out pan, add lemon juice and cream, then taste and adjust seasoning if necessary. Heat through thoroughly, but take care not to let the soup boil.

5 Pour the soup into 4 warmed individual soup bowls. Garnish each serving with a pepper ring and serve the soup at once.

Tomato rice soup

SERVES 4

1 lb fresh tomatoes, chopped

1 can (16 oz) tomatoes

1 tablespoon tomato paste

²/₃ cup water

salt and freshly ground black pepper

¹/₃ cup long-grain rice

2 tablespoons medium sherry

1 tablespoon finely chopped fresh parsley, for
   garnish

1 Put all the ingredients except the rice, sherry and parsley into a large saucepan. Bring to a boil, stirring, then lower the heat, cover and simmer for 30 minutes.

2 Pass the contents of the saucepan through a strainer, or let cool slightly, then purée in a blender and strain.

3 Pour the strained tomato purée back into the rinsed-out pan and bring back to a boil. Stir in the rice, lower the heat, cover and simmer for about 15 minutes or until the rice is tender.

4 Stir in the sherry, taste and adjust seasoning, then pour into warmed individual soup bowls. Sprinkle with parsley and serve at once.

Cheesy potato soup

SERVES 4

1¹/₂ lb potatoes, cut in even-size pieces

salt

2 tablespoons butter or margarine

1 large onion, finely minced

2 large cloves garlic, minced (optional)

3 celery stalks, finely chopped

1 large carrot, diced small

¹/₄ small rutabaga (weighing about 2 oz),
   finely diced

1¹/₄ cups vegetable stock

²/₃ cup milk

¹/₂ teaspoon dried thyme or marjoram

¹/₂ teaspoon celery salt

freshly ground black pepper

³/₄ cup shredded Cheddar cheese

3 tablespoons chopped fresh parsley

1 Cook the potatoes in boiling salted water to cover for about 15 minutes or until tender.

2 When the potatoes are cooked, let them cool slightly in the water, then

transfer both potatoes and water to a blender and blend until smooth. (If you do not have a blender, pass them through a strainer.) Return the purée to the rinsed-out pan.

3 Melt the butter in a large skillet, add the onion and garlic, if using, and sauté over moderate heat until beginning to soften. Add the remaining vegetables to the pan and cook, stirring occasionally, for about 10 minutes, until all the vegetables are soft, and the onion, celery and rutabaga are just beginning to color.

4 Mix the vegetables with the potato purée in the saucepan, then stir in the stock, milk, thyme and celery salt. Add pepper to taste.

5 Bring to a boil, lower the heat and simmer gently for about 15 minutes or until the vegetables are just soft. Stir in the cheese, reserving 2 tablespoons, and simmer for a further 2-3 minutes. Taste the soup and add salt and additional pepper if required.

6 Pour into a warmed soup tureen. Sprinkle with the chopped parsley and the reserved 2 tablespoons shredded cheese and serve at once. Pass extra shredded cheese separately if liked.

Celery and Stilton soup

SERVES 4

1 head celery, finely chopped
¼ lb Stilton cheese, trimmed of rind
3 tablespoons butter
2 large leeks, thinly sliced
3 cups vegetable stock
2 large egg yolks
¼ cup light cream
salt and freshly ground black pepper

For garnish

¼ cup vegetable oil
2 slices bread, crusts removed, cubed
4 teaspoons chopped fresh parsley

1 Melt the butter in a large, heavy-bottomed saucepan. Add the celery and leeks, cover and cook gently, stirring occasionally, for about 10 minutes, until the vegetables are soft but not colored.

2 Add the stock and bring to a boil. Lower the heat and simmer, uncovered, for about 20 minutes, until vegetables are tender. Cool slightly.

3 Meanwhile, make the croûtons:

Left: Tomato rice soup
Above: Celery and Stilton soup

Heat the oil in a heavy skillet over moderate heat until very hot, add the bread cubes and sauté until golden brown on all sides, turning them frequently. Drain well on absorbent kitchen paper and set aside.

4 Work the slightly cooled vegetable mixture to a purée in a blender. Return the soup to the rinsed-out pan and reheat gently, without bringing to a boil.

5 Meanwhile, beat the egg yolks and cream together until smoothly blended. In a separate bowl, mash the cheese to a coarse paste with a fork, then gradually work in the egg and cream mixture.

6 Stir a small ladleful of the hot soup into the cheese mixture, then pour the mixture back into the pan, stirring constantly until the soup has thickened slightly.

7 Pour the soup into 4 warmed individual bowls and garnish each with chopped parsley and the croûtons. Serve at once.

Appetizers

Our tasty appetizers range from unusual vegetable pâtés to exotic fritters – perfect for introducing a meal and excellent as melt-in-the-mouth snacks.

Herb pâté

SERVES 6

2 lb zucchini
1 tablespoon salt
1/4 cup butter
4 eggs
1 1/4 cups heavy cream
2 tablespoons chopped mixed fresh herbs, such as chervil, parsley, mint and tarragon
pinch of cayenne
freshly ground black pepper
vegetable oil, for greasing
hot French bread, to serve

For garnish

3 tablespoons heavy cream
extra chopped mixed fresh herbs
sprigs of fresh herbs
lettuce leaves
cucumber slices
tomato wedges

1 Preheat the oven to 350°F. Line a 2-quart loaf pan with paper, then grease the paper with oil.
2 Coarsely shred the zucchini into a colander. Sprinkle in the salt, stir well and set aside for 1 hour. Then strain, discarding the liquid which will have formed. Rinse the zucchini under cold running water and pat dry.
3 Melt the butter in a saucepan, add the zucchini and cook over a low heat for about 10 minutes, stirring occasionally, until they are soft. Let cool.
4 Put the eggs and cream in a bowl and mix well. Add the zucchini and butter mixture and the herbs. Stir well and season with a pinch of cayenne and black pepper to taste.
5 Pour the mixture into the prepared pan, cover with foil and stand in a roasting pan. Pour enough cold water to come halfway up the sides of the loaf pan.
6 Bake in oven for 1 1/4 hours until the pâté is firm. Leave the pâté to cool in the pan, then turn out onto a serving platter.
7 To serve: Whip the cream until it forms soft peaks, then spread over the top of the pâté. Scatter with chopped mixed fresh herbs and garnish with herb sprigs. Arrange the lettuce leaves, cucumber slices and tomato wedges around the edge of the serving platter.

Spinach pâté

SERVES 4

1/2 lb young spinach leaves, cooked, drained and finely chopped
2 tablespoons butter
6 scallions, finely chopped
2 tablespoons chopped fresh mint
1 tablespoon light cream
2/3 package (8 oz size) cream cheese
pinch of cayenne
1 tablespoon lemon juice
salt and freshly ground black pepper
4 thin lemon slices, for garnish
hot wholewheat rolls, to serve

1 Melt the butter in a pan, add the scallions and sauté gently for 2-3 minutes, stirring occasionally. Add the chopped mint and spinach and mix well. Remove from the heat and let cool.
2 When the spinach mixture is cool, stir in the cream, cream cheese, cayenne, lemon juice and salt and pepper to taste. Work the mixture in a blender until smooth.
3 Divide the pâté between 4 individual ovenproof dishes or custard cups and smooth surface of each. Cover and refrigerate for at least 1 hour.
4 To serve: Garnish with lemon slices and serve with hot rolls.

Gingered eggplant dip

SERVES 4

2 lb firm eggplants, stems removed
3/4 cup plain yogurt
1 clove garlic, minced
1 tablespoon light brown sugar
1 teaspoon grated fresh gingerroot
1/2 teaspoon cumin powder
salt and freshly ground black pepper
parsley sprigs, for garnish

1 Preheat the oven to 400°F. Prick the eggplants all over the surface with a fork, then put them into a roasting pan and bake in the oven for 45-60 minutes, until they feel really soft when they are pressed with the back of a spoon.
2 Remove the eggplants from the oven and let cool enough to handle. Cut them in half lengthwise, and squeeze gently in your hand to drain off the bitter juices. Scoop out flesh and leave until cold.
3 Put eggplant flesh in a blender with the yogurt, garlic, sugar, ginger, cumin and salt and pepper to taste. Blend until smooth. Transfer to 1 large or 4 small serving dishes. Refrigerate for 2-3 hours to allow dip to firm up.
4 Just before serving, garnish with parsley sprigs.

Luxurious Herb pâté

Lentil and orange purée

SERVES 4

1 cup split red lentils

2½ cups water

1 bay leaf

salt and freshly ground black pepper

juice of ½ small orange

2 tablespoons white wine vinegar

¼ cup vegetable oil

1 clove garlic, minced

4 large celery stalks, finely chopped

2 tablespoons chopped celery leaves (optional)

For garnish

2 small oranges, peeled and cut in sections

¾ lb tomatoes, thinly sliced

celery leaves

white mustard and garden cress

1 Put the lentils into a saucepan with the water, bay leaf and salt and pepper to taste. Bring to a boil, then lower the heat, cover and simmer for 45 minutes. Using a wooden spoon, stir occasionally at first, then more frequently toward the end so that the lentils are beaten to a thick purée.

2 Discard the bay leaf, then let the lentils cool in the covered pan for 1 hour.

3 Beat the orange juice, vinegar, oil and garlic into lentil purée. Taste and adjust seasoning, then mix in the chopped celery and the reserved chopped celery leaves, if using. Stir well.

4 Put the purée into the center of a serving platter and form it into a smooth mound with the back of a metal spoon. Garnish the purée with the orange sections and arrange the sliced tomatoes and celery leaves around the edge. Arrange the white mustard and garden cress near the tomatoes.

Potted Stilton

MAKES ABOUT 1½ LB

1 lb Blue Stilton cheese, rind removed

1 cup butter

pinch of salt

2 pinches of ground mace

2-4 tablespoons ruby or vintage port

1 Melt ½ cup of the butter in a small saucepan. Remove from the heat and allow the foam that has developed to fall gently to the base of the pan. Pour the clear butter into a bowl, taking care not to disturb the sediment. Set the clear butter aside.

2 Soften the remaining butter, then put in a mortar and pound with the cheese until evenly blended. Pound in the salt and mace. Work in enough port to give a good flavor and smooth texture; the cheese must not "weep".

3 Press the mixture into scalded custard cups, tapping on the table while filling to knock out any airholes. Leave ½ inch headspace.

4 Pour the clear butter in a thin layer on top of each cup, then refrigerate overnight.

5 To serve: Break and remove the butter coating. The butter-sealed cheese can safely be kept for up to 2 weeks.

Hummus

SERVES 4

⅔ cup dried chick-peas

¼ cup olive oil

1 large clove garlic, minced

¼ cup lemon juice

¼ cup tahini paste

salt and freshly ground black pepper

¼ teaspoon mild paprika

few sprigs of fresh parsley and lemon wedges, for garnish

1 Put the chick-peas into a deep bowl, cover them with plenty of cold water and let soak for several hours or overnight.

2 Drain and rinse the chick-peas, put them into a saucepan and cover with fresh cold water. Bring to a boil, then lower the heat and simmer for about 1 hour, until tender, adding more water to the pan during the cooking time if the chick-peas become too dry.

3 Drain, reserving the liquid; cool.

4 Reserve 12 chick-peas for garnish. Put the remainder into a blender with half the oil, the garlic, lemon juice, tahini paste and salt and pepper to taste. Blend to a smooth purée, adding a little of the reserved liquid if necessary to give a consistency like thick mayonnaise. Refrigerate for at least 1 hour.

5 To serve, spoon mixture into a shallow dish, or 4 small individual ones. Put the paprika into a small bowl and gradually stir in the remaining olive oil to make a smooth paste. Drizzle this over the top of the hummus, garnish with the whole chickpeas, parsley and lemon wedges.

Spicy bean pâté

SERVES 4

1 can (16 oz) red kidney beans
1 clove garlic, minced
1 tablespoon tomato paste
1 teaspoon soy sauce
1 teaspoon lemon juice
few drops of hot pepper sauce
salt and freshly ground black pepper
parsley sprigs, for garnish

1 Drain the beans, reserving the liquid from the can.
2 Put all the ingredients into a blender and blend to a smooth paste; it will be flecked with pieces of bean skin. Alternatively, place all the ingredients in a bowl, pound them with the end of a rolling pin, then mash thoroughly

with a fork. If the mixture becomes too thick, add 2-3 tablespoons of the reserved liquid from the can.
3 Taste and adjust seasoning.
4 Pack the pâté into 4 small ramekins or custard cups and carefully smooth the surface of each with a small knife. Serve the pâté cold or chilled, garnished with parsley sprigs.

Garlic dip with crudités

SERVES 4-6

1/2 lb young green beans, cleaned
1/2 lb zucchini, cut in 3 inch matchstick lengths
1 small cauliflower, broken into flowerets
1/2 lb young carrots, cut in 3 inch matchstick lengths
salt
Garlic dip
3-5 cloves garlic
1/2-3/4 teaspoon salt
2 egg yolks, at room temperature
7/8 cup olive oil, at room temperature
1-2 teaspoons lukewarm water
1 teaspoon lemon juice
pinch of freshly ground white pepper

1 Blanch the green beans in boiling

Left: Lentil and orange purée is delicious served with a wholegrain bread
Above: Garlic dip with crudités makes a colorful display

water for 1 minute, then immediately cool under cold running water, drain and reserve.
2 Dust the zucchini with salt; leave to sweat.
3 Make the dip: Crush the peeled garlic cloves and mash to a paste with the salt. Put the egg yolks in a bowl, add the garlic and salt paste, then, using a wire whip or rotary beater, beat until well combined.
4 Drop by drop, add the oil, beating thoroughly after each addition. When the mixture looks glossy, add the oil a little faster, but do not add too much or the mixture will separate. When the mixture becomes too thick to stir easily, beat in some lukewarm water to thin slightly.
5 Beat in the lemon juice and pepper to taste. Pour the dip into a small serving bowl and place in the center of a platter.
6 Pat the zucchini dry with absorbent kitchen paper. Surround the dip with the zucchini, beans, cauliflower and carrots and serve.

Avocado dip

SERVES 4-6

2 ripe avocados

juice of 1 lemon

1 clove garlic, minced (optional)

4 tomatoes, peeled, seeded and finely chopped

1 small onion, minced

4 tablespoons finely chopped celery

2-3 tablespoons olive oil

1 tablespoon chopped fresh parsley

salt and freshly ground black pepper

To serve

carrot and celery matchsticks

chips or cheese crackers

1 Cut the avocados in half lengthwise, remove the seeds, then scoop out the flesh with a teaspoon. Put the flesh in a bowl and mash it with a wooden spoon.

2 Add the lemon juice, garlic, if using, tomatoes, onion and celery.

3 Stir in enough olive oil to make a soft, smooth mixture, then add the chopped parsley and season to taste.

4 Transfer the dip to a serving bowl, cover with plastic wrap and refrigerate for 30 minutes. Serve with vegetable matchsticks and crackers.

Summer dip

SERVES 6

1 cup cottage cheese

2 tablespoons plain yogurt

2 scallions or ½ onion

4 gherkins, finely chopped

salt and freshly ground black pepper

dash of hot pepper sauce (optional)

cucumber and celery matchsticks, to serve

1 Strain or blend the cottage cheese until smooth.

2 Add the yogurt and mix well.

3 Wash and trim the scallions. Mince and add to the yogurt mixture. Add the finely chopped gherkins and stir to mix well.

4 Season to taste with salt and pepper and add hot pepper sauce, if using. Cover and refrigerate.

5 Just before serving, stir, transfer to a serving bowl and serve with a garnish of crisp cucumber and celery matchsticks.

Hot cauliflower terrine

SERVES 4

1 large cauliflower, broken into flowerets
salt
¼ cup butter
1 large onion, minced
1½ cups soft wholewheat bread crumbs
2 eggs, separated
2 tablespoons finely chopped fresh parsley
¼ teaspoon freshly grated nutmeg
freshly ground white pepper
⅔ cup heavy cream, lightly whipped
vegetable oil, for greasing

1 Preheat the oven to 375°C and grease a 9 × 5 inch loaf pan.
2 Bring a pan of salted water to a boil and cook the cauliflower for 10 minutes until tender. Drain well and mash until smooth.
3 Melt the butter in a pan, add the onion and sauté gently for 5 minutes until soft but not colored. Stir in the cauliflower purée, bread crumbs, egg yolks, parsley and nutmeg. Season generously with salt and pepper. Beat the egg whites until standing in stiff peaks and fold them in, together with the cream.
4 Transfer the mixture to the prepared loaf pan, then cover with waxed paper or foil. Bake in the oven for 1 hour.
5 Leave the terrine in the pan for 3 minutes, then turn out onto a warmed serving dish and serve at once.

Vegetable terrine

SERVES 4

12 large green cabbage leaves, central midribs removed
salt
1 carrot (weight about ¼ lb), cut in matchstick lengths
1 zucchini (weight about ¼ lb), cut in matchstick lengths
1 can (about 8 oz) corn and pimiento, drained
2 eggs, plus 1 egg yolk
⅔ cup milk
3 tablespoons heavy cream
¼ nutmeg, grated
freshly ground black pepper
vegetable oil, for greasing

Tomato sauce
½ lb tomatoes, roughly chopped
3 tablespoons plain yogurt
1 teaspoon Dijon mustard
1 teaspoon tomato ketchup
pinch of superfine sugar

1 Preheat the oven to 325°F.
2 Bring a saucepan of salted water to a boil and blanch the cabbage leaves for 2 minutes. Drain and dry on a clean dish towel.
3 Bring a saucepan of salted water to a boil, lower the heat and put the carrot and zucchini matchsticks in to simmer for 5 minutes. Drain and refresh under cold water, drain again.
4 Grease a 9 × 5 inch loaf pan with vegetable oil. Line the loaf pan with 3 or 4 of the largest cabbage leaves and chop the remainder fairly finely.
5 Put half the carrot and zucchini mixture into the lined loaf pan, add half the corn and pimiento, then half the chopped cabbage. Repeat the layering to make 6 layers in all.
6 Beat the eggs lightly with the extra yolk, milk, cream and nutmeg. Season with salt and pepper. Carefully pour the egg mixture into the loaf pan, gently easing the vegetables apart in several places with a round-bladed knife, to make sure the egg mixture is evenly distributed through the pan and goes right to the base. Fold any protruding cabbage leaves over the filling. Cover the pan with foil.
7 Set the loaf pan in a roasting pan. Pour in hot water to come three-quarters up the sides of the loaf pan and cook for 1½-2 hours, until the custard is set and firm to the touch. Remove the loaf pan from the roasting pan and cool. Chill the terrine overnight in the refrigerator.
8 To make the sauce: Put the tomatoes in a blender for a few seconds until puréed, then strain to remove the peels and seeds.
9 Mix this tomato purée with the remaining sauce ingredients, stirring to make sure they are well combined. Season to taste with salt and pepper. Cover with plastic wrap and chill for at least 2 hours.
10 To serve: Let the terrine stand at room temperature for about 10 minutes. Run a knife around the sides of the terrine, invert a serving platter on top and shake gently to unmold the terrine. Serve cut in slices with the tomato sauce.

Left: Avocado dip
Below: Vegetable terrine

Egg mousse

SERVES 4

3 hard-cooked eggs, yolks and whites separated
2 teaspoons agar-agar
2/3 cup vegetable stock
1¼ cups thick bottled mayonnaise
1-2 teaspoons curry paste
salt and freshly ground black pepper
1 egg white
parsley sprigs, for garnish

1 Sprinkle the agar-agar over the stock in a small pan, then stir to mix well. Boil until dissolved. Let the mixture cool slightly, then slowly beat the mixture into the mayonnaise until well blended.
2 Sieve the egg yolks and stir into the mayonnaise mixture with the curry paste. Chop the egg whites and fold two-thirds of them into the mixture. Season carefully with salt and pepper.
3 Beat the egg white stiffly and fold it into the mixture with a large metal spoon until evenly incorporated. Pour into 4 individual ovenproof dishes or custard cups that have been rinsed out with cold water.
4 Refrigerate for about 3 hours or until set.
5 To serve: Run a knife around the edge of each mousse and unmold onto small plates. Garnish with the remaining chopped egg white and parsley sprigs. Serve at once.
● The mousse can be made in a 4-cup soufflé mold.

Spanish vegetable omelet

SERVES 4

1 lb potatoes, cut in 1 cm/½ inch dice
salt
6 oz fresh green beans or ¼ lb frozen green beans
2 tablespoons vegetable oil
1 onion, chopped
1 sweet red pepper, seeded and diced
7 eggs, beaten
2 tablespoons finely chopped fresh parsley
½ teaspoon mild paprika
freshly ground black pepper
a little extra finely chopped fresh parsley, for garnish

1 Bring a pan of salted water to a boil and cook the potatoes for about 5 minutes, until just tender but not mushy. Drain, refresh in cold water and drain again. Put the potatoes in a large bowl.
2 If using fresh beans, bring a pan of salted water to a boil and cook them for about 8 minutes until tender but still crisp. If using frozen beans, cook for about 5 minutes. Drain, refresh in cold water and drain again. Cut the beans in 1-1½ inch lengths and add to the potatoes in the bowl.
3 Heat the oil in a large non-stick skillet, add the onion and red pepper and cook gently for about 5 minutes, stirring occasionally, until soft but not colored. Remove the onion and pepper from the pan with a slotted spoon, draining all the oil back into the pan, and add to the potatoes and beans in the bowl.
4 Add the beaten eggs, parsley and mild paprika to the vegetables in the bowl and stir lightly together. Season to taste with salt and pepper.
5 Reheat the oil in the pan over low heat and pour in the omelet mixture. Level out the vegetables and leave to cook very gently for 15-20 minutes, until the base is set but the top is still soft and creamy. Meanwhile, preheat the broiler to high.
6 Set the skillet under the broiler at the lowest position from the heat for 2-3 minutes, until the top of the omelet is set and light golden. Loosen the omelet from the pan with a slim spatula, then with a fish turner slide it carefully onto a large platter. Sprinkle lightly with chopped parsley and let cool slightly. Serve the omelet cut in wedges.

Stuffed eggs with green mayonnaise

SERVES 4

4 large hard-cooked eggs

about 1/4 teaspoon lemon juice

pinch of cayenne

*1/2-1 tablespoon finely chopped mixed fresh
    parsley, watercress and tarragon*

Green mayonnaise

1/3 cup parsley sprigs

1/4 cup watercress sprigs

salt

1 cup thick bottled mayonnaise

*1/2 tablespoon each finely chopped fresh
    parsley, watercress and tarragon*

freshly ground black pepper

*1/4-1/2 teaspoon lemon juice or wine vinegar
    (optional)*

1 Make the green mayonnaise: Carefully wash the parsley and watercress sprigs. Bring 1¼ cups salted water to a boil, plunge in the herbs, reduce heat and simmer for 6 minutes. Drain well, then pat the herbs as dry as possible in absorbent kitchen paper. Put them in a mortar and crush finely, then press through a strainer.

2 Reserve ¼ cup of the mayonnaise and blend the rest with the strained herbs. Stir in the finely chopped parsley, watercress and tarragon and season to taste with freshly ground black pepper, and a little lemon juice or wine vinegar, if liked. Refrigerate until ready to use.

3 Prepare the stuffed eggs shortly before serving, as the filling tends to discolor if left exposed to the air for too long. Carefully shell the hard-cooked eggs. Cut them in half lengthwise and scoop out the yolks, taking care not to break the whites.

4 Rub the egg yolks through a fine nylon strainer, then mix well with the reserved mayonnaise and season with the lemon juice and cayenne.

5 Cut a thin slice from the rounded side of each egg white half, if necessary, so that it will stand firmly. Fill each egg white with yolk mixture, piling it up and smoothing it over so that it resembles the whole egg.

6 Spread the green mayonnaise in a shallow rectangular serving dish large enough to take the stuffed eggs side by side. Arrange the eggs on the layer of mayonnaise and sprinkle with the finely chopped mixed green herbs. Serve at once.

Avocado pancakes

MAKES ABOUT 16

1 large firm avocado, pared and chopped

4 eggs

1 tablespoon milk

1 teaspoon salt

1 onion, chopped

1/3 cup all-purpose flour

1 large potato, shredded

1 tablespoon lemon juice

freshly ground black pepper

butter, for greasing

Sauce

1/2 cup sour cream

1/2 cup plain yogurt

dash of hot pepper sauce

freshly ground black pepper

1 Make the sauce: Put the sour cream in a bowl and beat in the yogurt, hot pepper sauce and black pepper to taste.

2 Put the eggs with milk, salt and chopped onion into the goblet of a blender and blend until thoroughly combined. Add the avocado, flour, potato, lemon juice and black pepper to taste and blend for a few seconds at low speed.

3 Preheat oven to 225°F.

4 Heat a heavy skillet over a moderate heat, lightly grease with butter and pour in about ¼ cup of the batter. Cook until the underside is lightly browned, then turn the pancake over and cook until browned on the other side. Carefully lift onto a sheet of waxed paper and keep warm in the oven.

5 Continue making pancakes in the same way, interleaving them with waxed paper.

6 Serve the pancakes with the sauce passed separately.

Left: Egg mousse and toast fingers
Below: Stuffed eggs with mayonnaise

Egg and spinach nests

SERVES 4

4 eggs

1/2 lb spinach, stems and large midribs removed, shredded

2 tablespoons butter or margarine

salt and freshly ground black pepper

1/4 cup heavy cream

cayenne, for garnish

margarine, for greasing

buttered wholewheat toast, to serve

1 Preheat the oven to 375°F. Grease 4 individual ovenproof dishes or custard cups.
2 Melt the margarine in a saucepan, add the spinach and cook gently for 8 minutes, or until soft. Season to taste with salt and pepper.
3 Divide the spinach among the prepared dishes. Break 1 egg into each dish on top of the cooked spinach mixture.
4 Place the dishes on a baking sheet and bake in oven for 10 minutes, until the egg whites begin to set. Remove from the oven and spoon 1 tablespoon cream over each egg. Return to the oven and cook for a further 5 minutes.
5 Sprinkle a little cayenne over each egg and serve at once with buttered wholewheat toast.

Egg and avocado bake

SERVES 6

6 eggs, separated

1 large avocado

6 tablespoons browned bread crumbs

3 tablespoons vegetable oil

1 onion, minced

1 clove garlic, minced (optional)

4 tablespoons finely chopped fresh parsley

salt and freshly ground black pepper

3/4 cup shredded Cheddar cheese

melted margarine, for greasing

finely chopped fresh parsley or coriander for garnish

1 Preheat the oven to 400°F. Brush 6 individual ovenproof dishes or custard cups with melted margarine, then coat them evenly with 4 tablespoons of the bread crumbs. Shake out the excess crumbs. Set aside.

Left: Egg and spinach nests
Above: Tomatoes with cheese filling

2 Heat the oil in a skillet, add the onion and garlic, if using, and sauté gently for 3-4 minutes until the onion is soft but not colored. Set aside to cool for about 5 minutes.

3 Cut the avocado in half. Remove the seed, scoop out the flesh into a bowl, then mash with a fork to a purée. Beat in the egg yolks and parsley, then the cooled onion and salt and pepper to taste.

4 Beat the egg whites until standing in stiff peaks, then fold them into the avocado mixture. Pile into the dishes, scatter remaining crumbs on top and bake in the oven for 20 minutes.

5 Sprinkle the top of the rising mixture with the cheese, then return dishes to the oven for a further 15 minutes until bakes are well risen and golden.

6 Garnish with the finely chopped parsley and serve at once.

Tomatoes with cheese filling

SERVES 4

8 fairly large, firm ripe tomatoes
2/3 package (8 oz size) cream cheese
2/3 cup small curd cottage cheese
2 tablespoons half-and-half or light cream
2 tablespoons finely chopped fresh parsley
2 teaspoons tomato paste
salt and freshly ground black pepper
8 sprigs of parsley, for garnish

Dressing

6 tablespoons vegetable oil
2 tablespoons wine vinegar
1/2 teaspoon dry mustard
1/2 teaspoon dried basil
2 teaspoons superfine sugar

1 Slice the tops off the tomatoes and reserve. Using a teaspoon, carefully scoop out the seeds and core.

2 Put the cheeses in a bowl with the half-and-half, parsley, tomato paste and salt and pepper to taste. Blend together. Spoon the mixture into tomatoes, piling it high, and replace the reserved tomato lids at an angle.

3 Place the stuffed tomatoes in a shallow dish. Beat together the dressing ingredients with a fork, adding salt and pepper to taste. Spoon the dressing over the tomatoes and chill in refrigerator for at least 30 minutes.

4 To serve: Put 2 tomatoes on each of 4 plates. Beat the dressing remaining in the dish together again and sprinkle 1 teaspoon of the dressing over each tomato. Tuck a sprig of parsley beneath the lid of each tomato for garnish.

Italian stuffed mushrooms

SERVES 4

16 large mushrooms

1/2 package (10 oz size) frozen finely chopped spinach

1 tablespoon olive oil

1/4 cup butter or margarine

1 small onion, minced

1 clove garlic, minced

1/2 cup Ricotta cheese or strained cottage cheese

4 tablespoons grated Parmesan cheese

4 tablespoons fresh wholewheat bread crumbs

salt

freshly ground black pepper

parsley sprigs, for garnish

garlic bread, to serve

1 Preheat the oven to 350°F. Cook spinach according to package directions.

2 Meanwhile, remove the stems from the mushrooms and set aside. (Use the mushroom stems for making stock.) Heat the oil and half the butter in a skillet, add the onion and garlic, and sauté them gently for 5 minutes until the onion is soft and lightly colored. Remove from heat.

3 Put the cooked spinach in a bowl with the Ricotta, Parmesan and bread crumbs. Stir in the onion and garlic, together with the buttery juices left in the pan, and season to taste with salt and pepper.

4 Place the mushrooms, gills uppermost, in an ovenproof dish and divide the stuffing equally among them. Dot with the remaining butter and bake in the oven for 15 minutes.

5 Using a fish turner, transfer the mushrooms to 4 warmed individual serving plates, garnish with sprigs of parsley and serve at once with garlic bread.

Above: Italian stuffed mushrooms
Right: Braised stuffed artichokes

Chinese lettuce parcels

SERVES 6

6 large crisp lettuce leaves

2 tablespoons vegetable oil

4 scallions, finely chopped

1 teaspoon ground ginger

1 celery stalk, finely chopped

3/4 cup finely chopped mushrooms

1/4 cup finely sliced canned water chestnuts

1 cup cooked long-grain rice

2/3 cup frozen peas, cooked and drained

1 1/2 tablespoons soy sauce

1 egg, beaten

extra soy sauce, to serve

1 Dip the lettuce leaves in boiling water for 10 seconds to soften, then drain on absorbent kitchen paper.

2 Heat the oil in a wok or large skillet. Add the scallions and ginger and sauté gently for 2-3 minutes until soft.

3 Add the celery, mushrooms and water chestnuts and cook for a further 5 minutes.

4 Stir in the rice, peas and soy sauce. Off heat, stir in the egg.

5 Lay the lettuce leaves out flat on a working surface. Put about 2 generous tablespoons of the mixture at the base of each lettuce leaf. Fold the leaf around the mixture and roll up to form neat parcels. Secure with toothpicks, if necessary.

6 Place the parcels in a steamer. If you do not have a steamer, use a metal colander which fits neatly inside a saucepan (the bottom must not touch the water). Fill the pan with boiling water, place the parcels in the colander and place the colander in the pan. Cover with foil or lid of steamer and steam for 5 minutes.

7 Remove the toothpicks from the parcels, if using, then place the parcels on a warmed serving dish. Serve at once, with extra soy sauce passed separately.

Braised stuffed artichokes

SERVES 4

4 globe artichokes
salt
1/2 lemon
1 tablespoon lemon juice
2 tablespoons butter
1 1/4 cups dry white wine
1 onion, minced
2 carrots, quartered

Stuffing

1/4 cup butter
1/2 cup chopped mushrooms
1 cup soft wholewheat bread crumbs
2 tablespoons chopped fresh parsley
2 teaspoons dried mixed herbs
2 cloves garlic, minced
finely grated rind of 1 lemon
freshly ground black pepper

1 Bring a large pan of salted water to a boil.

2 Meanwhile, prepare artichokes: Using a sharp knife, neatly cut off the artichoke stems, then slice off the top third of each artichoke. Discard the trimmings. Rub the cut surfaces with the lemon to prevent discoloration.

3 Using kitchen shears, trim any remaining sharp tips from the leaves, rub with lemon, then open them to expose the central whiskery "choke", surrounded by purple leaves. Pull out the purple leaves, then scoop out the hairy chokes with a teaspoon; discard.

4 Add the lemon juice to the boiling water and then add the artichokes and cook for 15-20 minutes or until an outer leaf of the artichokes can be pulled out quite easily.

5 Meanwhile, make the stuffing: Melt the butter in a saucepan, add the mushrooms and sauté gently for 5 minutes until soft and lightly colored. Transfer to a bowl and stir in remaining stuffing ingredients. Season to taste with salt and pepper and mix.

6 Drain the artichokes, then stand upside down in a colander to extract all the water.

7 Preheat the oven to 350°F.

8 Stand the artichokes upright and spoon the stuffing into the centers. Place in an ovenproof dish, then put a knob of butter on top of each.

9 Pour the wine around the artichokes, then add the onion and carrots to the wine. Season lightly with salt and pepper, cover the dish with foil and cook in the oven for about 40 minutes.

10 Serve at once, straight from the dish; pour a little wine sauce over each serving.

Spinach soufflés

SERVES 4

1 lb fresh spinach or 1 package (10 oz size)
  frozen chopped spinach

salt

¼ cup butter or margarine

1 onion, minced

¼ cup all-purpose flour

⅔ cup milk

good pinch of freshly grated nutmeg

freshly ground black pepper

4 eggs, separated

1 tablespoon grated Parmesan cheese

margarine, for greasing

1 If using fresh spinach, wash very thoroughly and remove the stems and central midribs. Place the spinach in a saucepan with only the water that clings to the leaves, and sprinkle with salt. Cover and cook over moderate heat for about 10 minutes until the spinach is cooked, stirring occasionally. If using frozen spinach, cook according to package directions.

2 Drain the spinach well in a strainer, pressing out all the excess water. Chop the spinach, if using fresh.

Grease four 1½-cup soufflé molds. Preheat the oven to 375°F.

3 Melt the butter in a large saucepan, add the onion and cook over low heat for about 5 minutes until soft and lightly colored. Sprinkle in the flour and stir over low heat for 1-2 minutes until straw-colored. Remove from the heat and gradually stir in the milk. Return to moderate heat and simmer, stirring until thick.

4 Stir in the chopped spinach and grated nutmeg and season well with salt and pepper. Simmer over gentle heat for 2 minutes.

5 Remove from the heat. Beat the egg yolks and beat them into the spinach mixture.

6 Beat the egg whites until they are just standing in soft peaks then beat 1-2 tablespoons into the spinach mixture. Carefully fold the rest of the whites into the mixture.

7 Pour the mixture into the greased soufflé molds and sprinkle the tops evenly with the grated Parmesan cheese. Bake in the oven for 20-30 minutes until risen and lightly browned on the top. They should be firm to the touch on the outside, and not wobbly if gently shaken, but still moist in the center. Serve at once.

Above: Spinach soufflés
Right: Mixed vegetables à la Grecque

Asparagus with walnuts

SERVES 4

1 lb asparagus, trimmed

salt

¼ cup walnut oil

pinch of cayenne

½ cup finely chopped walnuts

4 tablespoons finely chopped fresh parsley or
  coriander

1 Tie the asparagus in 4 bundles. Bring a deep pan of salted water to a boil and put in the asparagus, leaving the tips above the water. Cover with the lid or a dome of foil and boil gently for 15 minutes until tender.

2 Drain the asparagus and put each bundle on a warmed individual plate. Remove the twine.

3 Spoon walnut oil over each bundle and sprinkle with a little cayenne. Divide the chopped walnuts and the parsley among the plates and serve at once.

Potato gnocchi and tomato sauce

SERVES 4

1½ lb potatoes
1 cup all-purpose flour
2 tablespoons butter, softened
pinch of freshly grated nutmeg
1 egg yolk, beaten
½ cup grated Parmesan cheese
butter or margarine, for greasing
Tomato sauce
1 small onion, minced
1 clove garlic, minced (optional)
1 can (5 oz size) tomato paste
1½ cups water
1 teaspoon sugar
1 bay leaf
pinch of dried basil
salt and freshly ground black pepper

1 Make the sauce first: Place all the ingredients in a pan with salt and pepper to taste. Bring to a boil, then lower the heat, cover and simmer gently for 30 minutes.
2 Meanwhile, bring the potatoes to a boil in salted water, lower the heat and cook for 20 minutes until tender. Drain, then pass through a strainer into a bowl.
3 Work the sauce through a strainer, then return to the rinsed-out pan. Set aside. Grease an ovenproof dish and preheat oven to 225°F.
4 Beat the flour into the potatoes with the butter, nutmeg and salt and pepper to taste. Add just enough of the beaten egg yolk to bind the mixture. Work in ⅓ cup of the grated Parmesan cheese.
5 Bring a large pan of lightly salted water to the simmering point.
6 Meanwhile, turn the potato mixture onto a floured surface, divide into 3 and form each piece into a roll about 1 inch in diameter. Cut each roll in 1 inch slices.
7 Drop slices from 1 roll into the simmering water. Cook for about 5 minutes, or until they rise to the surface and look puffy. Remove with a slotted spoon, place in the prepared dish and keep hot in the oven while you cook the remaining pieces in the same way.
8 Reheat the tomato sauce. Preheat the broiler to high.
9 Pour a little of the warmed tomato sauce over the gnocchi and top with the remaining Parmesan. Place under the broiler for about 5 minutes until the top is golden and bubbling. Serve at once, with the remaining sauce passed separately in a warmed pitcher.

Mixed vegetables à la Grecque

SERVES 4

½ lb pearl onions
¾ lb frozen green beans, thawed
1½ cups thickly sliced button mushrooms
salt
2 tablespoons chopped fresh parsley
Sauce
6 tablespoons dry white wine or hard cider
¼ cup olive oil
¼ cup tomato paste
1 onion, thinly sliced
1 clove garlic, minced
1 teaspoon mustard seed or pickling spice
freshly ground black pepper

1 Bring a large pan of salted water to a boil and blanch the pearl onions for 3 minutes. Drain the pearl onions very thoroughly.
2 Make the sauce: Put the wine, oil, tomato paste, sliced onion, garlic and mustard seed into a large pan. Stir well and bring to a boil, then lower the heat, cover the pan and simmer over very low heat for 25 minutes, stirring the sauce once or twice. Season the sauce to taste with salt and freshly ground black pepper.
3 Add the whole onions, beans and sliced mushrooms to the sauce and return to a boil. Cover the pan, lower the heat and simmer for 20 minutes. Taste and adjust the seasoning, if necessary.
4 Remove from the heat and let cool, then transfer to a covered container. Stir in most of the fresh parsley and refrigerate for 30 minutes.
5 To serve: Sprinkle with remaining parsley for garnish and serve.

Above: Cheesy potato fritters
Right: Melted Mozzarella sandwiches

Oriental vegetable fritters

SERVES 4

1 large cauliflower, broken in bite-size florwerets
2 bunches green onions, cleaned and halved lengthwise
1 lb carrots, halved lengthwise and cut in 2¹/₂ inch lengths
vegetable oil, for deep-frying

Batter

1 cup all-purpose flour
¹/₄ teaspoon baking soda
¹/₄ teaspoon salt
¹/₄ teaspoon ground ginger
1 egg yolk
⁷/₈ cup water

Dipping sauce

3 tablespoons tomato paste
1¹/₂ tablespoons soy sauce
1¹/₂ tablespoons honey
¹/₄ cup vegetable stock

1 Make the dipping sauce: Stir together the ingredients for the sauce, then divide the mixture among 4 tiny dishes or custard cups. Set aside.
2 Make the batter: Sift the flour, soda, salt and ground ginger into a bowl. Beat the egg yolk with the cold water and add gradually to the flour, stirring with a wooden spoon to make a smooth thin batter.
3 Preheat the oven to 250°F. Heat the oil in a deep-fat fryer to 375°F, or until a cube of bread turns golden brown in 50 seconds.
4 Dip a few of the vegetable pieces into the thin batter. Transfer them to the hot oil with a slotted spoon and deep-fry for about 3 minutes or until golden brown, turning once with the spoon. Remove from the pan with the slotted spoon and drain well on absorbent kitchen paper. Arrange on a warmed large serving platter and keep warm in the oven while frying the remaining vegetables pieces in the same way.
5 Serve the fritters as soon as they are all cooked; provide each person with a bowl of sauce so that he can dip his vegetables into it.

Cheesy potato fritters

MAKES 20-24

2 lb potatoes
1 package(3¹/₂ oz) semi-soft cheese flavored with garlic and herbs
2 eggs
salt and freshly ground black pepper
vegetable oil, for frying
1 tablespoon chopped chives, for garnish (optional)

1 Shred the potatoes, then drain them in a colander lined with a dish towel. Gather the dish towel up and squeeze out as much liquid from the potatoes as possible.
2 Put the cheese into a bowl and beat with a wooden spoon until soft. Beat in the eggs, then mix in the potatoes and season the fritter mixture with salt and pepper to taste.
3 Preheat the oven to 225°F.
4 Pour enough oil into a deep skillet to cover the base to a depth of 1 inch. Heat the oil over moderate heat until

sizzling hot, then cook the potato mixture in batches; drop tablespoons of the mixture into the oil, spacing them well apart. Cook the fritters for about 3 minutes on each side until golden brown.

5 Remove from the pan with a slotted spoon, drain on absorbent kitchen paper, then transfer to a serving dish. Keep hot in the oven while cooking the remaining mixture in the same way. Serve the fritters as soon as they are all cooked, garnished with the chopped chives, if liked.

Melted Mozzarella sandwiches

SERVES 4

¼ lb Mozzarella cheese

8 large slices white or wholewheat bread

¼ cup butter, softened

freshly ground black pepper

3 eggs, beaten

vegetable oil, for frying

parsley sprigs, for garnish

1 Spread the bread with the butter and cut off the crusts with a sharp knife. Season 4 of the bread slices with pepper.

2 Cut the Mozzarella in thin slices and arrange them in a single layer on the seasoned bread, leaving a ¼ inch margin all around the edge of each slice of bread.

3 Top with the remaining 4 bread slices. Press the edges firmly together.

4 Put beaten eggs on a plate and dip in each sandwich to coat thoroughly all over. Make sure that the edges are well covered with egg so that they are sealed.

5 Preheat the oven to 225°F. Pour enough oil into a large skillet to come to a depth of ¼ inch. Heat gently until a bread cube sizzles and turns golden brown when carefully dropped into the oil.

6 Cook the sandwiches 2 at a time for 3-4 minutes on each side until golden brown.

7 Drain very thoroughly on absorbent kitchen paper. Keep warm in the oven while cooking the remaining sandwiches. Serve the melted Mozzarella sandwiches at once, garnishing each one with a small sprig of parsley.

Cheese beignets

SERVES 4

1½ cups shredded Gruyère cheese

3 eggs, separated

¼ teaspoon salt

¼ cup butter

6 tablespoons all-purpose flour

1 cup water

vegetable oil, for deep-frying

1½ cups shredded Gruyère cheese

¼ cup grated Parmesan cheese

1 Beat the egg yolks till frothy. In a clean, dry bowl, beat the egg whites until they stand in stiff peaks.

2 Melt the butter in a small saucepan. Sprinkle in the flour and stir over low heat for 1-2 minutes. Gradually stir in the water and simmer, stirring, until thick and smooth. Remove from the heat.

3 Heat the oil in a deep-fat fryer to 350°F; or until a cube of bread turns golden brown in 60 seconds.

4 Beat the Gruyère cheese into the hot sauce. Fold in the beaten whites.

5 Fry 1 tablespoon of batter, a few at a time, turning once with a slotted spoon. When golden, remove and drain on absorbent kitchen paper. Sprinkle with Parmesan and serve.

Walnut croquettes

MAKES ABOUT 16

1 cup very finely chopped walnuts
1¹/₂ cups soft wholewheat bread crumbs
¹/₂ small onion, minced
¹/₂ cup shredded Edam cheese
1 tablespoon finely chopped fresh parsley
salt and freshly ground black pepper
1 large egg, lightly beaten
1-2 tablespoons milk
2 tablespoons vegetable oil, for frying

Sauce

1 tablespoon butter or margarine
¹/₂ package (10 oz size) frozen spinach
²/₃ cup sour cream
freshly grated nutmeg

1 Put the walnuts in a bowl with the bread crumbs, onion, cheese, parsley and salt and pepper to taste. Stir in the beaten egg, then add just enough milk to bind the mixture together. Form into about 16 balls, using your hands.
2 To make the sauce: Melt the margarine in a small saucepan, add the spinach and heat gently for about 10 minutes until thawed, stirring frequently. Drain thoroughly in a strainer, pressing out the liquid with a saucer, then chop with a knife. Return to the pan, stir in the sour cream, then season to taste with nutmeg and salt and pepper. Set aside.
3 Heat the oil in a skillet, add the croquettes and sauté them carefully for about 10 minutes, turning them frequently until brown on all sides.
4 Meanwhile, gently heat the sauce until hot, but do not boil. Spoon the sauce into a warmed serving bowl and place in the center of a large platter. Arrange the croquettes on the platter around the sauce, and serve at once.

Mushroom and cheese pirozhki

MAKES 24

2 tablespoons butter
1 cup finely chopped mushrooms
1 scallion, finely chopped
1 package (3¹/₂ oz) semi-soft cheese, flavored with garlic and herbs
¹/₂ teaspoon dillweed
salt and freshly ground black pepper
pie dough, made with 1 cup wholewheat flour (page 42)
1 egg yolk, lightly beaten, for glaze
vegetable oil, for greasing
parsley sprigs, for garnish

1 Preheat the oven to 350°F and grease a baking sheet with oil.
2 Melt the butter in a skillet and gently sauté the mushrooms and scallion for 3 minutes. Remove from heat and cool.
3 In a clean, dry bowl, mash the soft cheese with the dillweed. Stir in the mushrooms and scallion, season to taste with salt and pepper, then cool in a refrigerator.
4 Meanwhile, roll out the dough on a lightly floured working surface to a ¹/₄ inch thickness. Using a round dough cutter or the rim of a glass, cut out circles approximately 3¹/₂ inches in diameter.
5 Place 1 teaspoonful of the mushroom and cheese mixture on one half of each circle, taking care not to overfill the dough circles or they will be very difficult to seal. Fold into a crescent shape and seal edges with water. Continue until all are filled.
6 Place crescents on prepared baking sheet and then brush each one with a little egg yolk to glaze. Bake in the oven for 30-40 minutes until the pastry is cooked and light golden in color. Transfer to a warmed serving platter, garnish with the parsley and serve.

French onion flan

SERVES 6

2 large onions, minced
1/2 cup butter
1 tablespoon all-purpose flour
3 eggs
2/3 cup light cream
2/3 cup heavy cream
pinch of freshly grated nutmeg
salt and freshly ground black pepper
finely sliced onion rings or parsley sprigs, for garnish
margarine for greasing

Cheese pastry

1 1/2 cups all-purpose flour
1/2 teaspoon dry mustard
1/2 teaspoon salt
pinch of cayenne
1/2 cup diced butter
3/4 cup shredded Cheddar cheese
1 large egg yolk, lightly beaten
4-5 teaspoons water

1 Make the dough: Sift the flour, dry mustard, salt and cayenne into a bowl. Add the butter and cut into the dried ingredients with your fingertips, until the mixture resembles fine bread crumbs. Stir in the Cheddar cheese. Mix to a stiff paste with the egg yolk and water.

2 Turn the dough out onto a lightly floured surface and knead gently until smooth. Wrap the dough in plastic wrap and chill in the refrigerator for at least 30 minutes.

3 Preheat the oven to 400°F. Grease a 9 inch loose-bottomed pie pan or flan ring set on a baking sheet.

4 Roll out the dough on a lightly floured surface and use to line the pie pan or flan ring. Prick the base of the dough all over with a fork. Line the pie shell with foil and fill it with baking beans. Bake in the oven for 10 minutes, then remove from the oven. Lower the oven temperature to 350°F.

5 Remove the foil and baking beans, then bake the pie shell for a further 5

Left: Mushroom and cheese pirozhki are excellent with thin soup
Above: French onion flan has a rich cheese pie shell

minutes to crisp slightly.

6 Meanwhile, make the filling: Melt the butter in a small pan, add the onions and sauté gently for 10 minutes until soft. Remove the pan from the heat and let the onions cool.

7 Stir in the flour, then beat together the eggs and light and heavy cream and beat into the onion mixture. Add the nutmeg and season to taste with salt and pepper.

8 Lower the oven temperature to 325°F. Pour the filling into the pie shell and bake for 35-40 minutes, until set and golden brown.

9 Let the flan cool for about 5 minutes, then carefully remove from the pan or ring and transfer to a serving platter. Garnish with the onion rings and serve warm or cold.

Tomato, cheese and basil flan

SERVES 4-6

4 large tomatoes, each weighing about ½ lb, sliced

1¼ cups milk

3 large eggs

1½ teaspoons dried basil

¾ cup shredded sharp Cheddar cheese

freshly ground black pepper

a few tomato slices, for garnish (optional)

Wholewheat pie dough

1 cup wholewheat flour

½ teaspoon baking powder

pinch of salt

¼ cup butter or margarine, diced

2-3 tablespoons cold water

1 Make the dough: Sift the flour with the baking powder and salt, then tip the bran left in the strainer onto the flour and stir in well. Add the margarine and cut into the flour with your fingertips until the mixture resembles fine bread crumbs. Mix in just enough cold water to form a soft ball. Wrap the dough in plastic wrap and place in the refrigerator for 30 minutes.

2 Preheat the oven to 375°F.

3 Roll out the dough on a floured surface and use to line an 8 inch loose-bottomed pie pan or flan ring set on a baking sheet.

4 Arrange the tomato slices overlapping in the pie shell. In a bowl, beat together the milk, eggs, basil, ½ cup of the cheese and salt and black pepper to taste.

5 Pour the mixture into the pie shell and sprinkle over the remaining cheese. Bake in the oven for 40-45 minutes until the filling is set and golden brown on top.

6 Let the flan cool for 5 minutes, then carefully remove from pan and transfer to a serving platter. Garnish the edge with tomato slices, if liked. Serve warm or cold.

*Right: **Tomato, cheese and basil flan** is full of flavor*
*Far right: **Watercress flan** has a light cottage cheese filling*

Spinach nut pasties

MAKES 8

1¼ packages (10 oz size) frozen spinach, thawed

3 tablespoons vegetable oil

2 onions, chopped

¼ cup porridge oats

1 cup finely chopped mixed nuts

2 teaspoons soy sauce

salt and freshly ground black pepper

pie dough, made with 2 cups wholewheat flour (see left)

vegetable oil, for greasing

1 Make the filling: Heat the oil in a pan, add the onions and sauté gently for 5 minutes until soft and lightly colored. Add the porridge oats and continue cooking for about 5 minutes until lightly colored. Off heat, stir in the spinach, nuts and soy sauce. Season with salt and pepper to taste, then leave until completely cold.

2 Preheat the oven to 400°F. Lightly grease a baking sheet with vegetable oil.

3 Divide the dough into 8 equal portions and roll out each portion to a 4 inch round. Using a tablespoon, divide the spinach filling among the pastry rounds, placing a portion in the middle of each one.

4 Brush halfway around the dough edges with water. Gently lift the dough sides and bring them up to meet in the middle and enclose the filling completely. Seal the edges firmly and crimp.

5 Arrange the pasties on the prepared baking sheet. Prick the tops of the pasties and cover the baking sheet with foil.

6 Bake the pasties in the oven for 25-30 minutes until crisp and lightly browned. Serve hot or cold.

Watercress flan

SERVES 6

2 bunches of watercress, finely chopped
pie dough made with 1 cup wholewheat flour (page 42)
1½ cups cottage cheese, strained
3 eggs, beaten
3 tablespoons milk
pinch of cayenne
salt and freshly ground black pepper
lightly beaten egg white, to seal
watercress sprigs, for garnish

1 Preheat the oven to 400°F.

2 Roll out the dough on a lightly floured surface and use to line an 9 inch pie pan. Prick base with fork. Place a large circle of waxed paper or foil in the pie shell and weight it down with baking beans. Bake pie shell for 10 minutes.

3 Remove the paper or foil lining and beans, brush the pie shell with beaten egg white, then return to the oven for a further 5 minutes.

4 Meanwhile, make the filling: Put the strained cottage cheese into a large bowl, add the chopped watercress, beaten eggs and milk and mix well with a fork. Add the cayenne and season with salt and pepper.

5 Spoon the filling into the cooked pie shell and spread evenly.

6 Return to the oven for about 45 minutes, or until the filling has set and is golden brown on top. Serve flan garnished with the watercress sprigs.

Brie quiche

SERVES 4-6

pie dough, made with 1 cup wholewheat flour (page 42)
lightly beaten egg white, to seal
watercress sprigs, for garnish

Filling

½ lb Brie cheese, rind removed and reserved and cut in 1 inch squares
⅔ cup light cream
3 eggs
½ teaspoon light brown sugar
pinch of ground ginger
pinch of ground turmeric
pinch of salt

1 Preheat the oven to 400°F.

2 On a lightly floured surface, roll out the dough to line an 8 inch loose-bottomed pie pan or flan ring set on a baking sheet. Prick the base lightly with a fork. Place a large circle of waxed paper or foil in the pie shell and weight it down with baking beans. Bake in the oven for 10 minutes.

3 Remove the beans and paper or foil, brush the inside of the pie shell with beaten egg white and return the pie shell to the oven for a further 5 minutes to crisp slightly.

4 Meanwhile, put the cheese in a blender with the remaining filling ingredients and blend until smooth.

5 Lower the oven temperature to 350°F. Arrange the squares of Brie rind over the base of the pie shell and pour over the filling. Bake in the oven for 30-40 minutes, until the filling is set and brown. The squares of rind rise to the top of the filling and melt to form a golden crust over the top of the quiche.

6 Let the quiche cool for about 5 minutes, then carefully remove from pan and transfer to a serving platter. Garnish the center with watercress sprigs and serve warm or cold.

Main Courses

Vegetables, grains, eggs and cheese are miraculously transformed into delicious vegetarian main courses. Plan your menu around the main course to ensure a well-balanced meal.

Cauliflower and oat casserole

SERVES 4

1 cauliflower, broken into flowerets
1 cup rolled oats
salt
2 tablespoons all-purpose flour
1¼ cups sour cream
1 teaspoon prepared mild yellow mustard
1½ cups shredded sharp Cheddar cheese
freshly ground black pepper
2¼ cups trimmed button mushrooms
2 tablespoons butter
½ cup roughly chopped walnuts

1 Preheat the oven to 400°F. Put the cauliflower flowerets in a saucepan containing 1 inch of boiling salted water and cook for about 7 minutes, or until they are just tender. Drain the cauliflower well

2 Meanwhile, put the flour in a small bowl and mix to a smooth paste with a little of the sour cream. Gradually stir in the remaining sour cream, the mustard, half the shredded cheese and salt and freshly ground black pepper to taste.

3 Mix in the cauliflower and mushrooms, turning gently so that all the vegetables are coated. Pour into a shallow ovenproof dish.

4 Using a fork, mix the butter with the oats, then add the rest of the cheese and the walnuts to make a lumpy, crumbly mixture.

5 Sprinkle the oat mixture evenly over the cauliflower and mushrooms and bake for 40 minutes until the topping is golden brown and crisp. Serve at once.

Ratatouille

SERVES 6

3 large eggplants, halved lengthwise
3 large zucchini, halved lengthwise
salt
⅔ cup olive oil
3 large onions, sliced in thin rings
¼ cup tomato paste
4 cloves garlic, chopped
3 large peppers, seeded and cut in strips
5 large tomatoes, peeled and chopped
1 tablespoon chopped fresh coriander
small pinch of cinnamon
1 teaspoon chopped fresh basil
freshly ground black pepper

1 Cut the eggplants and zucchini across in slices about ¾ inch thick, then arrange them in layers in a colander, sprinkling each layer with salt. Top with a weighted plate and let vegetables drain for 1 hour.

2 Heat the oil in a large heavy-bottomed pan over low heat, add the onions and sauté for about 10 minutes until soft but not colored. Stir in the tomato paste and cook for 3-4 minutes.

3 Rinse the eggplants and zucchini, then pat dry with absorbent kitchen paper. Stir them into the pan. Add the garlic and the peppers, shake the pan, cover and simmer for 20 minutes.

4 Add the tomatoes and the rest of the seasoning, stir, and leave to cook for a further 40-45 minutes. Remove the lid for the final few minutes to let the sauce reduce if it seems too liquid.

5 Taste and adjust the seasoning. Transfer to a warmed dish and serve the ratatouille hot, or serve cold.

Bulgarian vegetable stew

SERVES 4

½ cup dried navy beans, soaked overnight
½ cup whole brown lentils, soaked overnight
2 tablespoons vegetable oil
2 large onions, chopped
2 teaspoons ground cumin
2 teaspoons ground coriander
4 sweet red peppers, seeded and sliced
1 quart unsalted vegetable stock or water
¼ cup tomato paste
⅓ cup dried currants
salt and freshly ground black pepper
sugar

1 Heat the oil in a large Dutch oven, add the onions, cumin and coriander and cook gently for 5 minutes, until soft. Add the peppers and cook gently for 4-5 minutes, stirring from time to time.

2 Drain the navy beans and boil rapidly in water for 10 minutes; drain. Drain the lentils, then add with the beans to the onions and peppers. Stir well, then pour in the vegetable stock. Add the tomato paste and currants and stir well.

3 Bring to a boil, then lower the heat and simmer, half-covered, for 1-1¼ hours, until the lentils and beans are tender and the sauce is thick.

4 Season to taste with salt, freshly ground black pepper and a little sugar. Serve the Bulgarian vegetable stew very hot, with hunks of crusty bread, if liked.

Hearty Bulgarian vegetable stew

Vegetable hotpot

SERVES 4

1 large onion, thinly sliced

1½ cups sliced carrots

2 tablespoons butter or margarine

2½ cups hot vegetable stock or water

1 tablespoon tomato paste

bouquet garni

salt and freshly ground black pepper

2 cups sliced leeks

⅔ cup diced parsnips

1½ cups cubed potatoes

*shredded Cheddar cheese and chopped fresh
   parsley, to serve*

1   Melt the butter in a large saucepan, add the onion and sauté gently for 5 minutes, until soft and lightly colored. Add the carrots and stir for 1 minute. Pour on the stock, add the tomato paste and bouquet garni and season to taste with salt and pepper. Stir well to mix.

2   Bring to a boil, cover, lower the heat slightly and simmer gently for 10 minutes.

3   Add the leeks and parsnips and cook for a further 10 minutes. Add a little extra boiling water if the sauce seems to be drying out.

4   Add the potatoes to the saucepan, cover and cook for a further 30 minutes, or until all the vegetables are tender.

5   Discard the bouquet garni, taste the stock and adjust the seasoning. Transfer the vegetables to a warmed serving dish and serve at once with the Cheddar cheese and parsley passed separately in small bowls.

Vegetable crisp

SERVES 4

2 leeks, cut in ½ inch slices

2 large carrots, thickly sliced

1 small sweet red pepper, seeded and diced

1 lb zucchini, cut in ½ inch slices

1 can (16 oz) tomatoes

2 tablespoons olive oil or sunflower oil

½ teaspoon dried basil

salt and freshly ground black pepper

¼-½ cup pine nuts (pignoli)

2 teaspoons wine vinegar

Topping

*1 cup all-purpose or wholewheat
   flour*

¼ teaspoon salt

3 tablespoons butter, diced

generous ½ cup grated fresh Parmesan cheese

1   Heat the oil in a large saucepan, add the leeks and carrots and sauté over moderate heat for 5 minutes, stirring. Add the red pepper and cook for 5 minutes, then add zucchini and sauté, stirring, for a further 5 minutes.

2   Add the tomatoes and their juices to the pan with the basil and salt and pepper to taste. Bring to a boil, then lower the heat, cover and simmer for 10 minutes.

3   Meanwhile, preheat the oven to 400°F and make the topping: Sift the flour and salt into a bowl. Add the butter and rub into the flour with the fingertips until the mixture resembles bread crumbs. Stir in all but 2 tablespoons of the Parmesan. Add pepper to taste.

4   Add the pine nuts and vinegar to the vegetables. Transfer to a 7-cup ovenproof dish. Sprinkle topping over vegetables. Top with reserved Parmesan.

5   Bake for about 40 minutes. Serve.

Vegetables in curry sauce

SERVES 4

1 small cauliflower, broken in flowerets
1½ cups thickly sliced scraped small carrots
1½ cups French beans, trimmed and halved
1½ cups hulled fava beans
salt
Sauce
2 tablespoons butter
¼ cup all-purpose flour
1 tablespoon mild curry powder
large pinch of ground ginger
1¼ cups milk
2 tablespoons fresh orange juice
freshly ground black pepper
2 tablespoons light cream or half-and-half
To serve
1 tablespoon blanched almonds, halved and
    toasted
1 tablespoon finely chopped fresh mint or
    parsley

1 Preheat the oven to 225°F.
2 Bring a large pan of boiling salted water to a boil, add all the prepared vegetables and cook until they are just tender – no more than 10 minutes. Do not let the vegetables become soft.
3 Drain the vegetables, reserving the stock, and transfer them to a warmed serving dish. Keep them hot in the preheated oven.
4 Make the sauce: Melt the butter in a saucepan, sprinkle in the flour and stir over low heat to form a paste. Stir in the curry powder and ginger and stir the paste constantly over moderate heat for 3 minutes.
5 Off heat, gradually stir in the milk, orange juice and 1¼ cups of the reserved stock. Return to the heat and simmer, stirring, for 3 minutes until thickened and smooth. Taste the sauce and season with pepper, and salt if necessary. Remove the pan from the heat and stir in the light cream or half-and-half.
6 Pour the sauce over the vegetables, lightly tossing them with a fork to coat well. Scatter with the almonds and chopped mint or parsley and serve at once.

● To toast the almonds, spread the nuts out in a broiler pan and broil under moderate heat until golden, shaking the pan occasionally. Watch the almonds closely all the time they are broiling, as they burn very easily.

Creamy spring vegetables

SERVES 4

1 small onion, sliced
2 large scallions, cut in ½ inch slices
2 carrots, cut in ½ inch slices
¼ cup butter
1¼ cups hot vegetable stock
pinch of superfine sugar
salt and freshly ground black pepper
½ lb fava beans (hulled weight)
½ lb peas (shelled weight)
1 teaspoon cornstarch
6 tablespoons heavy cream

1 Melt the butter in a saucepan, add the sliced onion and scallions and cook over moderate heat for 2 minutes. Add the sliced carrots and cook for a further 2 minutes, stirring to coat thoroughly.
2 Pour the hot stock into the pan, add the sugar and salt and pepper to

Left: Vegetable hotpot is based on a variety of root vegetables
Above: Creamy spring vegetables go well with plain brown rice

taste, then bring to a boil. Lower the heat, cover and simmer gently for 10 minutes. Add the fava beans and simmer for a further 5 minutes. Add the peas and continue simmering for another 10 minutes, until all the vegetables are tender.
3 Put the cornstarch into a small bowl and stir in 1 tablespoon of the hot liquid from the pan. Stir to make a smooth paste, then pour back into the pan. Stir the contents of the pan over low heat for about 4-5 minutes, until the sauce thickens and clears. Stir in the cream and allow just to heat through. Do not let the cornstarch sauce boil.
4 Turn the vegetables with the sauce into a warmed serving dish and serve at once.

Pumpkin stew

Vegetable cobbler

SERVES 4

1 lb pumpkin, pared, seeded and cut in ¾ inch cubes
3 tablespoons vegetable oil
1 onion, chopped
1½ cups thinly sliced carrots
½ cup red lentils
1 can (16 oz) tomatoes
1¼ cups vegetable stock
½ teaspoon ground mace
salt and freshly ground black pepper
⅔ cup sour cream, to serve

1 Heat the oil in a saucepan and sauté onion and carrots over moderate heat for 5 minutes.

2 Add the lentils, tomatoes with their juice, stock and mace, and season with salt and pepper to taste. Bring to a boil, lower the heat, cover the pan and simmer gently for 15 minutes.

3 Add the pumpkin to the pan, cover and then simmer gently for a further 15 minutes.

4 Taste and adjust the seasoning if necessary. To serve: Spoon the stew into warmed individual bowls, top each serving with a spoonful of sour cream and serve at once.

SERVES 4-6

1 lb Jerusalem artichokes, peeled and cut in 1 inch chunks
salt
¼ cup butter or margarine
1 onion, finely sliced
1 cup sliced mushrooms
⅓ cup all-purpose flour
1¼ cups milk
1 cup shredded Cheddar cheese
freshly ground black pepper
½ lb tomatoes, peeled and quartered

Topping

1½ cups wholewheat flour
1 tablespoon baking powder
½ teaspoon salt
3 tablespoons butter, diced
¼ cup finely chopped walnuts
¾ teaspoon dried mixed herbs
about ⅔ cup milk

1 Put the artichokes in a saucepan, cover with water and add a good pinch of salt. Bring to a boil, lower the heat slightly and simmer for 5-10 minutes until just tender. Drain, reserving the liquid.

2 Melt the butter in a saucepan, add the onion and sauté gently for 5 minutes until soft and lightly colored. Add the mushrooms and continue cooking for 5 minutes. Transfer the vegetables to a plate.

3 Sprinkle the flour into the pan and stir over low heat for 1-2 minutes. Off heat, gradually stir in ⅔ cup of the reserved artichoke liquid and the milk. Return to the heat and simmer, stirring, until the sauce is thick and smooth. Reserve 1 tablespoon of the cheese and stir the rest into the sauce. Season to taste with salt and freshly ground black pepper.

4 Stir in the artichokes, onion and mushrooms and tomatoes. Taste and adjust the seasoning, then turn the mixed vegetable mixture into a 7-cup casserole.

5 Preheat the oven to 425°F.

6 Make the biscuit topping: Sift the flour, baking powder and salt into a large bowl. Tip the bran left in the strainer into the bowl and stir well to mix. Add the butter and rub it in with the fingertips until the mixture resembles fine bread crumbs. Add the walnuts and herbs and gradually mix in enough milk to form a soft dough.

7 Turn the dough onto a lightly

floured surface and roll out thinly. Cut into about 15 rounds using a 2 inch cutter and arrange these on top of the casserole. Sprinkle with the reserved cheese.

8 Bake the casserole in the oven for about 30 minutes or until the biscuit topping has risen and is golden brown. Serve the vegetable cobbler at once, piping hot.

Mixed bean casserole

SERVES 4-6

$1/2$ cup navy beans
$1/2$ cup Egyptian brown beans
$1/2$ cup black-eyed peas
1 green pepper, seeded
2 tablespoons vegetable oil
1 large onion, chopped
1 small head of celery, chopped
2 cloves garlic, minced (optional)
1 can (about 1 lb 12 oz) tomatoes
2 cups water
1 teaspoon brewers' yeast
2 teaspoons dried oregano
salt and freshly ground black pepper

1 Put the navy beans into one bowl and the brown beans and black-eyed peas together in another. Cover both of them with cold water and let soak overnight.

2 Drain the navy and brown beans and black-eyed peas, rinse under cold running water, then put into a medium-size saucepan and cover with fresh cold water.

3 Bring to a boil and then boil for 15 minutes to remove any toxins. Lower the heat slightly, then cover the pan and continue cooking for a further 30 minutes.

4 Meanwhile, cut a few slices from the green pepper and reserve for the garnish. Chop the remaining pepper. Heat the oil in a large heavy-bottomed pan and gently sauté the onion, celery, the chopped green pepper and garlic, if using, for 10 minutes. Add the tomatoes and water, then stir in the brewers' yeast, oregano and salt and freshly ground black pepper to taste. Bring to a boil.

5 Drain the beans, add to the pan of vegetables, cover and cook gently for 1 hour or until the beans are very tender. Taste and adjust the seasoning, if necessary.

6 Transfer the beans to a warmed serving dish and serve at once, garnished with the reserved green pepper rings linked together.

Fruit curry

SERVES 4

1 banana
$1/2$ honeydew melon, cut in 1 inch cubes
1 cup each green and purple grapes, halved and seeded
1 orange, divided into sections
1 red eating apple, cored (do not pare)
$1/2$ cup creamed coconut, broken in small pieces
2 tablespoons curry paste
$2/3$ cup sour cream
plain boiled rice, to serve

1 Put the coconut, curry paste and sour cream into a large saucepan. Stir over low heat until the mixture is well blended.

2 Peel the banana, cut in $1/2$ inch slices and add to pan with the melon, grapes and orange. Cook gently, stirring, for 3-4 minutes until the fruit is warm.

3 Cut the apple in small wedges and remove cores. Stir into the pan and warm through.

4 Spoon the curry onto a bed of boiled rice and serve at once, while piping hot.

Above: Country goulash
Right: Rich potato pie

Country goulash

SERVES 4

2 tablespoons vegetable oil
2 onions, sliced
2 carrots, sliced
2 celery stalks, sliced
2 zucchini, sliced
1 green pepper, seeded and diced
1/2 cup sliced mushrooms
5-6 cups finely shredded hard white
   cabbage
1 can (16 oz) tomatoes
1 tablespoon tomato paste
1 teaspoon lemon juice
1 1/4 cups water
4 1/2 teaspoons mild paprika
1 tablespoon caraway seeds
salt and freshly ground black pepper
2/3 cup sour cream

1 Heat the oil in a large saucepan,
add the onions, carrots and celery and
sauté for about 5 minutes until soft and
lightly colored.
2 Add zucchini, green pepper,
mushrooms and white cabbage and
cook over moderate heat for 10 minutes, stirring occasionally to prevent
the vegetables sticking to the pan.
3 Stir in the tomatoes with their
juice, the tomato paste, lemon juice
and water. Sprinkle in the paprika and
caraway seeds and stir gently. Season
well with salt and freshly ground black
pepper.
4 Cover the pan and simmer for 20
minutes or until the vegetables are just
tender. Taste and add more seasoning
if necessary.
5 Transfer the goulash to a hot serving dish and spoon over the sour
cream. Serve at once.

Beet slice

SERVES 4-6

1 cup all-purpose flour
1 cup wholewheat flour
1/4 teaspoon salt
1/2 cup butter, diced
4-6 teaspoons ice water
Filling
1 1/2 cups shredded Lancashire cheese
1 cup coarsely shredded cooked beets
1 small onion, minced
1 teaspoon Dijon mustard
2 tablespoons thick bottled mayonnaise
1 tablespoon sweet pickle
salt and freshly ground black pepper

1 Make the dough: Sift both flours
into a bowl with the salt. Tip the bran
left in the strainer into the bowl and
stir to mix. Add the butter and rub
into the flours with your fingertips

until the mixture resembles fine crumbs. Add the water gradually and mix well to make a fairly firm dough that is not too dry and crumbly. Wrap the dough in plastic wrap and refrigerate for 30 minutes.

2 Preheat the oven to 400°F.

3 Meanwhile, make the filling: In a bowl mix together the cheese, beets, onion, Dijon mustard, mayonnaise, pickle and salt and pepper to taste. Stir thoroughly.

4 Roll out half the dough on a lightly floured surface and use to line a shallow 8 inch square pan. Roll out the remaining pastry into a square slightly larger than the top of the pan and set aside.

5 Spread the filling over the dough in the pan. Dampen the edges of the dough with water, then lay the reserved dough square over the top. Press it onto the side of the dough lining above the level of the filling, then trim the dough level with the top of the pan.

6 Brush with cold water, sprinkle lightly with salt, then make a vent in the top for the steam to escape. Bake just above the center of the oven for 30-35 minutes, or until the top is crisp and light golden.

7 Serve hot, warm or cold, cut in slices or squares.

Rich potato pie

SERVES 6

4 cups all-purpose flour

1½ teaspoons salt

⅞ cup butter, diced

2 eggs, separated

⅓ cup water

margarine, for greasing

Filling

2 lb waxy potatoes

salt and freshly ground black pepper

4 tablespoons chopped fresh parsley

2 tablespoons chopped fresh chervil or 2 teaspoons dried chervil

¾ cup finely chopped shallots

⅔ cup heavy cream, lightly whipped

1 Sift the flour and salt into a bowl and cut in the butter until the mixture resembles bread crumbs. Lightly beat one whole egg and one egg white with ¼ cup water, add to the dry ingredients and mix with a knife until the dough leaves the side of the bowl clean. Wrap the dough in plastic wrap and refrigerate for about 30 minutes.

2 Meanwhile, cook the potatoes for 5 minutes in a large pan of boiling, salted water. Drain well, and when cool enough to handle, cut in slices.

3 Preheat the oven to 400°F. Grease a 9 inch deep pie pan.

4 Roll out slightly more than half the dough on a lightly floured surface and use to line the prepared pan.

5 Arrange a third of the potato slices in the pie shell, season lightly with salt and pepper and sprinkle over half the herbs and shallots. Cover with another third of the potato slices, season and sprinkle with the rest of the herbs and shallots, then cover with the remaining potato.

6 Beat the remaining egg yolk with 1 tablespoon water and use to brush the dough edges. Roll out the remaining dough into a round slightly larger than the top of the pan, then place over the filled pan. Trim and seal the edges. Brush with the remaining egg yolk mixture and cut 4 small vents, spaced evenly, in the top of the pie, to allow the steam to escape.

7 Bake in the oven for 25 minutes, then lower the temperature to 350°F and cook for 20 minutes more.

8 Remove the pie from the oven and open the steam vents sufficiently with a sharp knife to take a small funnel. Pour one quarter of the cream into each of the steam vents and return the pie to the oven for a further 10 minutes, or until the top is rich golden brown. Serve at once.

Bulgur wheat casserole

SERVES 4

2 cups bulgur wheat

1/4 cup butter or margarine

1 tablespoon vegetable oil

1 large onion, minced

2 large leeks, thinly sliced

2 large carrots, diced

1 sweet red pepper, seeded and diced

1 1/4 cups boiling water

2 tomatoes, peeled and chopped

1/4 cup seedless raisins

1/4 lb Cheddar cheese, diced

salt and freshly ground black pepper

1 Melt half the butter with the oil in a large heavy-bottomed saucepan. Add the onion, leeks, carrots and red pepper, cover and cook gently for about 20 minutes.

2 Meanwhile, melt the remaining butter in a large saucepan. Add the bulgur wheat and stir until the grains are thoroughly coated with butter.

3 Stir in the boiling water, cover and place over gentle heat. Cook for 10 minutes until the water has been absorbed.

4 Using a fork, gently mix the cooked vegetables into the bulgur wheat. Lightly stir in the tomatoes, seedless raisins and diced cheese and fork through until the cheese is melted. Season to taste with salt and freshly ground black pepper.

5 Transfer the Bulgur wheat casserole to a warmed serving dish and serve at once.

Above: Bulgur wheat casserole
Right: Nutty rissoles

Chestnut wine loaf

SERVES 4-6

3/4 lb dried chestnuts or 2 lb fresh chestnuts

1/4 cup butter, plus extra for greasing

1 large onion, chopped

2 celery stalks, finely chopped

2 cloves garlic, minced

2 tablespoons chopped fresh sage

1 tablespoon red wine

1 egg

salt and freshly ground black pepper

1 sage leaf, for garnish (optional)

1 If using dried chestnuts, cover them with boiling water, let soak for at least 2 hours, then simmer in plenty of water for about 1½ hours until tender. For fresh chestnuts, nick each one with a knife, then simmer the chestnuts in plenty of water for about 10 minutes until the cuts open. Remove the chestnuts from the water one by one and strip off the skins with a sharp, pointed knife. Put the skinned chestnuts into a saucepan, cover with water and simmer for 20-30 minutes until tender. Drain and mash the chestnuts.

2 Preheat the oven to 350°F. Line the base and narrow sides of a 7 × 3 inch loaf pan with a long strip of non-stick parchment and brush with butter.

3 Melt the butter in a large saucepan, add the onion and celery and sauté gently for 10 minutes until soft but not colored. Remove from the heat. Add the mashed chestnuts, garlic, sage, wine and egg and mix well. Season with salt and freshly ground black pepper to taste.

4 Place the sage leaf, if using, in the base of the prepared loaf pan and spoon the chestnut mixture on top. Smooth over the surface with a spatula and cover with a piece of foil.

5 Bake the loaf in the oven for 1 hour. To serve: Slip a knife around the sides of the loaf and invert it onto a warmed serving dish. Serve the loaf at once.

Nutty rissoles

MAKES 12

2 cups mixed unsalted nuts, finely chopped
2 tablespoons butter
1½ cups finely chopped onions
1 large clove garlic, minced (optional)
1½ cups finely chopped mushrooms
2 cups soft wholewheat bread crumbs
1 tablespoon finely chopped fresh parsley
2 teaspoons dried mixed herbs
2 tablespoons tomato paste
1 teaspoon soy sauce
1 egg, beaten
salt and freshly ground black pepper
3-4 tablespoons all-purpose flour, for coating
vegetable oil, for frying
mushroom slices and walnut halves, for garnish
fried onion rings and tomato sauce (page 37), to serve

1 Melt the butter in a saucepan, add the onions and garlic, if using, and cook over gentle heat for 4-5 minutes until soft.

2 Remove the pan from the heat and stir in the nuts, mushrooms, bread crumbs, parsley and mixed herbs until well blended. Add the tomato paste and soy sauce and sufficient beaten egg to bind the mixture together. Season to taste with salt and pepper.

3 Roll heaped tablespoons of the mixture in flour to form 12 balls, then flatten them into rissoles about 3 inches in diameter.

4 Arrange the prepared rissoles on a floured baking sheet and leave in the refrigerator or in a cold place for about 1 hour.

5 Preheat the oven to 225°F.

6 Heat a little vegetable oil in a large skillet and cook half the rissoles, cooking them for about 5 minutes on each side or until crisp and golden brown. Remove with a slotted spoon; drain on absorbent kitchen paper. Put them in the oven to keep warm while cooking the remaining rissoles.

7 When all the rissoles are cooked, garnish with mushroom slices and walnut halves and serve them at once, with onion rings and tomato sauce.

Mixed vegetable croquettes

MAKES 16

2 onions, minced
6 celery stalks, minced
2 carrots, shredded
1½ cups minced mushrooms
1 tablespoon vegetable oil
1 tablespoon smooth peanut butter
½ cup unsalted peanuts, ground or very finely chopped
1½ cups soft wholewheat bread crumbs
pinch of dried mixed herbs
salt and freshly ground black pepper
2 eggs, beaten
¾ cup dry bread crumbs
vegetable oil, for deep-frying

1 Heat 1 tablespoon oil in a large saucepan, add the onions and celery and sauté gently for 5 minutes. Do not let vegetables brown.
2 Add the carrots and mushrooms to the pan and continue cooking for a further 5 minutes, stirring from time to time.

3 Off heat, stir in the peanut butter until well combined. Add the peanuts, wholewheat bread crumbs, herbs and salt and pepper to taste. Mix well and bind with half the beaten eggs. Let stand until cool enough to handle.
4 Meanwhile, pour the remaining beaten eggs into a shallow bowl or onto a plate. Place the dry bread crumbs on a separate plate, ready to coat the croquettes.
5 When the mixture is cool, divide it into 16 portions and shape them into croquettes. Dip each croquette in the beaten eggs, then roll in the bread crumbs until thoroughly coated.
6 Pour enough vegetable oil into a deep-fat fryer to come to a depth of 1½ inches. Heat to 350°F or until a 1 inch bread cube browns in 60 seconds. Lower in the croquettes and deep-fry for 3 minutes, until golden brown. Drain the croquettes thoroughly on absorbent kitchen paper and serve at once.

Below: Mixed vegetable croquettes
Right: Potato pizza

Soy burgers

SERVES 4

1 cup soy beans
2 tablespoons vegetable oil
1 onion, minced
1 small carrot, shredded
1 small green pepper, seeded and chopped
1 tablespoon tomato paste
1 teaspoon dried mixed herbs
salt and freshly ground black pepper
1 egg
1 tablespoon water
dry bread crumbs, for coating
vegetable oil, for frying

1 Put the beans into a bowl, cover with plenty of cold water and let soak overnight. Drain the soaked beans and put them into a saucepan; cover with cold water.
2 Bring the beans to a boil, then lower the heat and simmer over very gentle heat for 3 hours until tender, topping up with more water if necessary. Transfer to a colander and drain thoroughly.
3 Heat the oil in a skillet and gently sauté the onion and carrot for 5 minutes, until the onion is soft and lightly colored. Add the green pepper and sauté for a further 5 minutes, until the vegetables are just tender.
4 Add the beans, tomato paste and herbs to the pan, mashing the beans with a spoon to make the mixture hold together. Season with salt and pepper to taste.
5 Divide the mixture into 8 and shape each piece into a neat, flat circle. Beat egg and water together in a shallow bowl and spread bread crumbs out on a plate. Dip the burgers first into the beaten egg mixture, then into the dry bread crumbs, making sure they are well coated.
6 Preheat the oven to 225°F.
7 Heat the vegetable oil in a large skillet, add 4 burgers and cook over moderately high heat for 3 minutes on each side until crisp and browned. Place on a serving platter, and keep warm. Fry the remaining burgers in the same way and serve at once.

Potato pizza

SERVES 4

1½ cups cold mashed potatoes
1 cup self-rising flour
salt
¼ cup butter or margarine
vegetable oil, for greasing

Topping

1 tablespoon vegetable oil
1 large onion, sliced
1 sweet red pepper, seeded and sliced
1 clove garlic, minced (optional)
1 cup sliced button mushrooms
pinch of oregano
2 teaspoons malt vinegar
freshly ground black pepper
1 tablespoon tomato paste
6 oz Cheddar cheese, sliced
12 green olives, pitted (optional)

1 Preheat the oven to 450°. Grease a large baking sheet.
2 Make the crust: Sift the flour and salt into a large bowl. Add the butter and rub it in with your fingertips until the mixture resembles bread crumbs, then add the mashed potatoes and knead the mixture lightly until smooth.
3 Press the dough into a 10 inch round and refrigerate.
4 Meanwhile, make the topping: Heat the oil in a skillet, add the onion, red pepper and garlic, if using, and sauté gently for 5 minutes, until the onion is soft and lightly colored. Off heat, stir in the mushrooms, oregano, vinegar and salt and pepper to taste.
5 Place the potato crust on the baking sheet and spread the tomato paste over it, then top with the onion mixture. Arrange the cheese slices over the top and top with pitted olives, if liked.
6 Bake in the oven for 25-30 minutes or until the crust is firm and the cheese is golden brown. Serve at once.

● For a more pronounced Italian flavor, use sliced Mozzarella cheese instead of Cheddar and top with ripe olives. Basil or marjoram may be used in place of oregano.

Carrot and nut roast

SERVES 4

1½ cups coarsely grated carrots
1 cup cashew nuts or pieces
1 cup walnut pieces
4 oz (about 4 slices) granary or wholewheat bread
¼ cup butter or margarine
1 onion, finely chopped
6 tablespoons hot vegetable stock
2 teaspoons brewers' yeast
1 teaspoon honey
1 teaspoon dried mixed herbs
2 teaspoons lemon juice
salt and freshly ground black pepper
butter or margarine for greasing

1 Preheat the oven to 350°F. Grease a 4-cup shallow ovenproof dish. Grind the cashews, walnuts and bread together in batches in a blender until they are all fairly fine. Tip them into a bowl.
2 Melt the butter in a saucepan, add the onion and cook gently for 5 minutes until soft and lightly colored. Add the carrots and cook, stirring, for a further 5 minutes. Remove from the pan with a slotted spoon and add to the nuts and bread.
3 Put the hot stock in a bowl, add the brewers' yeast and honey and stir until dissolved. Stir into the nut mixture with the herbs and lemon juice. Taste the mixture and season with salt and pepper.
4 Spoon mixture into prepared dish and bake in the oven for 45 minutes. Serve the roast hot or cold, straight from the dish.

Herb and spinach crêpes

SERVES 4-6

1/2 cup all-purpose plain flour
1/2 teaspoon salt
2 eggs, beaten
2/3 cup milk
4-6 tablespoons water
1/3 cup melted butter
3/4 package (10 oz size) frozen chopped spinach, thawed
2 tablespoons finely chopped fresh basil, chives or tarragon
2-4 tablespoons grated Parmesan cheese
vegetable oil, for frying
butter, for greasing
tomato sauce (page 37), to serve

Filling

2 cups cottage cheese
1/2 cup sour cream
2 eggs, beaten
1/2 cup shredded Gruyère cheese
2-4 tablespoons grated Parmesan cheese
2-4 tablespoons finely chopped fresh herbs (parsley, chives and, when available, tarragon)
salt and freshly ground black pepper
freshly grated nutmeg

1 Make the batter: Sift the flour and salt into a bowl, then make a well in the center. Beat in the eggs, then gradually add the milk, water and 2 tablespoons of the melted butter. Stir gently until smooth.

2 Strain the batter through a fine strainer; it should be the consistency of light cream. Add a little water if too thick. Stir in the spinach and herbs and let stand for two hours.

3 Make the filling: Put the cottage cheese in a bowl with the sour cream, eggs, Gruyère and Parmesan cheeses and the herbs. Season to taste with salt, pepper and nutmeg. Refrigerate for 1 hour.

4 Make the crêpes: Heat a little oil in a heavy-bottomed 7 inch skillet over moderate to high heat. Pour off the excess. Beat the batter.

5 Off heat, pour about 2 tablespoons batter into the pan, then tilt the pan to spread the batter all over the base.

6 Return to the heat and cook until the underside is golden brown, then turn the crêpe and cook on the other side for a further 20-30 seconds until golden brown. Lift onto a sheet of waxed paper.

7 Continue making crêpes in this way, greasing the pan with more oil if necessary. Stack by interleaving with waxed paper, letting them cool.

8 Preheat the oven to 350°F. Spread each crêpe with 4-5 tablespoons of the filling, then roll up the crêpes and arrange in a greased baking dish.

9 Brush the crêpes with the remaining melted butter and sprinkle with the grated Parmesan cheese. Bake for about 20 minutes, until the crêpes are heated through. Serve at once, with the tomato sauce.

Nutty brown rice

SERVES 4

1 cup plus 2 tablespoons brown rice
2 1/2 cups water
1 teaspoon salt
2 tablespoons vegetable oil
1 large onion, chopped
2 celery stalks, finely chopped
1 bunch scallions, trimmed and chopped
1 red-skinned eating apple, cored and finely chopped
1/3 cup raisins
1/2 cup slivered almonds
1/2 cup roasted peanuts
steamed spinach, to serve

Cheese sauce

3 tablespoons butter
1/4 cup flour
1 1/4 cups milk
1 tablespoon mild, wholegrain mustard
1 cup shredded Cheddar cheese
freshly ground black pepper

1 Put the rice, water and salt in a heavy-bottomed saucepan and bring to a boil. Stir once, cover, and cook over a gentle heat for 40-50 minutes, or until the rice is tender and all the water has been absorbed.

2 Meanwhile, make the sauce: Melt two-thirds of the butter in a saucepan, sprinkle in the flour and stir over low heat for 1-2 minutes until straw-colored. Off heat, gradually stir in the milk. Return to the heat and simmer, stirring until thick and smooth. Stir in the mustard and cheese and season to taste with salt and pepper. Dot the remaining butter over the top of the sauce and set aside.

3 Heat the oil in a skillet, add the onion and celery and sauté gently for 10 minutes, taking care not to let them brown. Add the scallions and cook for a further 2 minutes.

4 Mix the vegetables into the cooked rice with a fork, then stir in the apple, raisins, almonds and peanuts. Heap the mixture onto a warmed serving dish and keep warm while you reheat the sauce, stirring in the butter on its surface.

5 To serve: Surround the rice with a ring of spinach, pour the cheese sauce over the top and serve thee nutty brown rice at once.

Moors and Christians

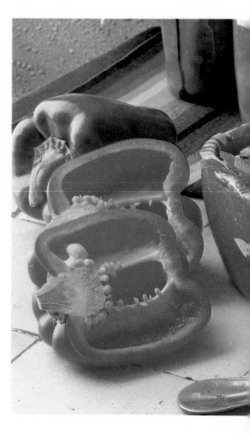

Spicy vegetable pilau

SERVES 6

2 cups Basmati rice, rinsed and drained
2 onions
1 inch piece fresh gingerroot
3 cardamom pods
3 cloves
1 inch length of cinnamon stick
¼ cup butter
1 small cauliflower, broken into flowerets
1 bay leaf (optional)
3-4 carrots, cut in matchstick strips
⅓ cup hulled peas
1¾ pints water
1 tablespoon sugar
salt
2 hard-cooked eggs, quartered, for garnish

1 Slice one of the onions lengthwise very thinly and reserve. Chop the other onion with the ginger and reserve. Crush the cardamom pods, cloves and cinnamon with a rolling pin and reserve.

2 Heat 1 tablespoon of the butter in a deep skillet or saucepan over moderate heat. When hot, sauté the cauliflower flowerets until they are light brown, then remove with a slotted spoon and set aside.

3 Add the rest of the butter to the pan and cook the onion slices until they are browned, then remove from the pan and set aside.

4 In the same fat, gently cook the onion and ginger mixture and the bay leaf, if using, until the onion is soft and lightly colored. Stir in the reserved spices, carrot strips and the peas, then add the rice and cook for about 5 minutes until it becomes transparent.

5 Add the water to the pan, together with the sugar and salt to taste. Bring the mixture to a boil, then lower the heat slightly and simmer for about 10 minutes or until the rice is half cooked.

6 Add the reserved cauliflower and continue cooking until the water is absorbed and the rice and vegetables are tender but not mushy.

7 Serve the pilau hot, garnished with the onion slices and the hard-cooked egg quarters.

Moors and Christians

SERVES 4-6

1⅓ cups black beans, soaked overnight and drained
2 tablespoons vegetable oil
1 onion, chopped
1 clove garlic, minced
1 green pepper, seeded and thinly sliced
1 sweet red pepper, seeded and thinly sliced
2 large tomatoes, peeled, seeded and chopped
1¼ cups long-grain rice
2½ cups water
large pinch of cayenne
salt and freshly ground black pepper
2 tablespoons butter
4-6 large eggs
1 tablespoon chopped fresh parsley

1 Rapidly boil the beans in unsalted water for 10 minutes. Cover with fresh water, bring to a boil, lower the heat and simmer for 1 hour.

2 Heat the oil in a saucepan, add the onion and garlic and sauté gently for 3 minutes until soft but not colored. Add the sliced peppers, stir well and fry for a further 3 minutes, stirring occasionally. Do not let the vegetables brown.

3 Add the tomatoes, rice, water, drained beans, cayenne and salt and pepper to taste. Stir well, cover the pan and simmer very gently for about 45 minutes, until the rice is tender and the liquid has been absorbed. Taste and stir in more salt, pepper and cayenne if necessary.

4 Preheat the oven to 225°F.

5 Spoon the rice mixture onto a warmed serving dish and keep warm. Heat the butter in a skillet and fry the eggs.

6 To serve: Divide the rice among 4-6 warmed serving plates and top each portion with a fried egg. Sprinkle each fried egg with parsley and serve at once.

8 Line the base and sides of the dish with half the blanched cabbage leaves, arranging them so that they overlap and letting them overhang the dish. Stir the cheese and egg into the rice mixture, season to taste with salt and pepper, then spoon into the lined dish. Level the surface of the mixture and cover with the remaining leaves. Fold over the overhanging leaves.

9 Cover the dish tightly with foil and cook in the oven for 45 minutes.

10 Loosen the sides with a knife and turn out onto a warmed platter. Serve at once.

Squash with nut stuffing

SERVES 4

1 whole squash (about 3 lb)

salt

¼ cup vegetable oil

1 large onion, finely chopped

1 clove garlic, minced

2 cups soft wholewheat bread crumbs

½ cup peanuts, shelled, skinned and ground

¾ cup ground cashew nuts

2 tablespoons finely chopped fresh parsley

1 tablespoon finely chopped fresh marjoram

1 tablespoon tomato paste

6 tablespoons dry white wine

freshly ground black pepper

vegetable oil, for greasing

1 Preheat the oven to 400°F. Lightly grease a casserole large enough to hold the squash in one piece.

2 Cut off both ends of the squash and reserve. Scoop and discard the seeds from the main part.

3 Put the squash and both reserved ends into a large saucepan of lightly salted boiling water, return to a boil, lower the heat and simmer for 5 minutes. Drain the squash well.

4 Heat the oil in a skillet over low heat, add the onion and garlic and sauté gently for 5 minutes until soft but not colored.

5 Off heat, mix in the bread crumbs, nuts, herbs, tomato paste and wine. Season to taste with salt and pepper.

6 Fill the squash with the stuffing, then fix the end pieces back in place with wooden cocktail picks. Place the squash in the casserole, cover and cook in the oven for 1 hour.

7 To serve: Discard the ends and cut the squash into 4 thick slices.

Stuffed cabbage pie

SERVES 4-6

1 green cabbage, weighing about 2 lb

1 orange

salt

1 cup long-grain rice

1 tablespoon butter or margarine

1 onion, chopped

1 tart apple, weighing about 5 oz

⅓ cup chopped dates

¾ cup shredded Cheddar cheese

1 egg, beaten

freshly ground black pepper

margarine, for greasing

1 Grate the rind of half the orange and squeeze the juice from the whole orange. Reserve.

2 Preheat the oven to 350°F and grease an ovenproof dish 8 inches in diameter and 3 inches deep.

3 Bring a saucepan of salted water to a boil and cook the rice for about 10 minutes until just tender.

4 Meanwhile, remove about 8 outer leaves of the cabbage and cut off any thick hard midribs. Bring another pan of salted water to a boil and blanch the cabbage leaves for 4 minutes. Drain and set aside. Chop the remaining cabbage and reserve.

5 Melt the butter in a large saucepan, add the onion and cook gently for 5 minutes until soft.

6 Add the chopped cabbage to the pan and cook over moderate heat, stirring, for 5 minutes. Pare, core and chop the apple and add to the pan. Cook for a further minute.

7 Drain the rice thoroughly and add to the pan with the dates, orange rind and juice. Remove from heat.

Sunflower seed peppers

SERVES 4

¼ cup sunflower seeds, toasted

2 large green peppers, halved lengthwise and seeded

2 tablespoons sunflower oil

1 large onion, chopped

1 sweet red pepper, seeded and cut in ½ inch squares

1 lb tomatoes, peeled and chopped

1 cup quartered button mushrooms

½ teaspoon dried thyme

¼ teaspoon mild paprika

salt and freshly ground black pepper

⅓ cup roughly shredded Edam or Gouda cheese

1 Heat the oil in a medium saucepan, add the onion and cook gently for 5 minutes until soft and lightly colored. Add the red pepper and cook for a further 2 minutes, stirring. Add the tomatoes, mushrooms, toasted sunflower seeds, thyme, paprika and salt and pepper to taste, then cook over a moderate heat for 10 minutes, stirring

Left: Stuffed cabbage pie
Below: Sunflower seed peppers

constantly until the mixture is thick.

2 Meanwhile, bring a saucepan of salted water to a boil. Put in the green pepper halves, bring back to a boil, lower the heat and simmer for 6 minutes until they are just tender. Drain thoroughly.

3 Preheat the broiler to high. Put the green pepper halves on the broiler rack and season them inside with salt and pepper. Pile the sunflower seed mixture into the pepper halves, pressing it down with a spoon. Sprinkle the cheese lightly on top.

4 Broil for a few minutes, until the cheese has melted. Transfer to warmed individual plates and serve.

Stuffed eggplants

SERVES 4

2 large eggplants

salt and freshly ground black pepper

¼ cup olive oil

2 onions, chopped

2 cloves garlic, minced

1 lb tomatoes, peeled and chopped

1 teaspoon dried basil

3 tablespoons chopped fresh parsley

1 tablespoon lemon juice

chopped fresh parsley, for garnish

1 Trim the eggplants, halve them lengthwise and scoop out the flesh, leaving a shell about ¼ inch thick. Sprinkle the insides of the shells thickly with salt and leave them in a colander to drain. Chop the scooped out flesh coarsely, add to the colander and salt too. Leave to drain for 1 hour.

2 Rinse the salt off the eggplants and dry the chopped flesh and the shells on absorbent kitchen paper. Preheat the oven to 350°F.

3 Heat 2 tablespoons oil in a skillet, add the onion and garlic and cook for about 10 minutes, until the onion is soft. Add the chopped eggplant flesh and the tomatoes, with any juice they may have made. Season the mixture well and cook gently for about 15 minutes, until the eggplant is soft. Stir in the basil and chopped parsley and remove from the heat.

4 Put the eggplant shells in an ovenproof dish and spoon the cooked mixture into them.

5 Sprinkle the remaining olive oil and the lemon juice over the filling and bake for about 1 hour, until the flesh on the shells is tender.

6 Remove the eggplants from the oven and let cool, then refrigerate for about 1 hour before serving. Transfer to a serving platter and garnish with chopped parsley.

Cheesy cornmeal pie

SERVES 4

1 generous cup cornmeal

salt

3 tablespoons vegetable oil

2/3 cup hot water

1 large onion, chopped

3 celery stalks, chopped

1 tablespoon tomato paste

freshly ground black pepper

1 cup shredded Cheddar cheese

4 tomatoes, peeled and sliced

6-8 stuffed olives, sliced

melted margarine, for greasing

1 Preheat the oven to 350°F. Grease the base and side of a 9 inch loose bottomed pie pan.
2 Place the cornmeal, pinch of salt and 2 tablespoons vegetable oil in a bowl and pour on the hot water. Stir well, then mix with your fingers to form a smooth, soft dough.
3 Line the prepared pie pan with the warm dough, gently kneading it into place with your fingers. Let cool.
4 Heat the remaining oil in a skillet. Add the onion and sauté gently for 5 minutes until soft and lightly colored. Add the celery and cook gently for another 10 minutes, stirring occasionally. Stir in the tomato paste and season to taste with salt and freshly

ground black pepper.
5 Sprinkle about one-third of the cheese evenly over the cornmeal base, then add the onion and celery mixture. Top with another third of the cheese. Arrange the sliced tomatoes on top, then sprinkle over the remaining cheese. Bake in the oven for about 35 minutes until the topping is golden.
6 Remove the pie from the oven, arrange the sliced olives decoratively on top, then return to the oven for a further 5 minutes. Remove from pan and serve hot.

● Mushrooms make a good addition to this pie. Add 1 cup sliced mushrooms with the celery.

Swiss cheese fondue

SERVES 6

3 cups coarsely shredded Gruyère cheese
3 cups coarsely shredded Emmental cheese
1 clove garlic, halved
2 teaspoons cornstarch
2 teaspoons Kirsch
2 cups dry white wine
2 teaspoons lemon juice
pinch of white pepper
freshly grated nutmeg

To serve

1 large French loaf, cut in 1 inch cubes
cocktail onions
pickled gherkins

1 Rub around the inside of a fondue pot with the cut sides of the garlic. Put the cornstarch in a small bowl and blend in the Kirsch until smooth.
2 Pour the wine and lemon juice into the fondue pot, place over a moderate heat and bring almost to the boiling point.
3 Off heat, gradually stir in the shredded cheeses.
4 Add the Kirsch mixture, together

Left: Swiss cheese fondue
Below: Cheese and chive soufflé

with the pepper and a sprinkling of nutmeg, stirring constantly until smooth. (If the mixture seems too thick, add a little more warmed white wine and stir well to mix.)
5 Carefully transfer the pot to its burner and stand. To serve: Guests spear a cube of bread onto a fondue fork and dip it into the hot fondue. Serve with onions and gherkins.

● It is best to use an earthenware or enameled iron fondue pot. If using a stainless steel fondue pot, make sure it has a thick base, as cheese is inclined to catch and burn if not watched.

Cheese and chive soufflé

SERVES 4

1¼ cups finely shredded Cheddar cheese
1 tablespoon chopped chives
¼ cup butter or margarine
1 small onion, finely chopped
6 tablespoons all-purpose flour
pinch of dry mustard
pinch of cayenne
1¼ cups milk
4 large eggs, separated
salt and freshly ground black pepper
melted margarine, for greasing

1 Brush the inside of a 5-cup soufflé mold with melted margarine. Preheat the oven to 350°F.
2 Melt the butter in a saucepan, add the onion and cook gently for about 5 minutes until soft and lightly colored but not browned.
3 Sprinkle the flour, mustard and cayenne into the pan and stir over low heat for 2 minutes.
4 Off heat, gradually stir in the milk. Return to the heat and simmer, stirring, until the sauce is thick and smooth.
5 Off heat, stir in the shredded cheese, then let sauce cool slightly. Beat the egg yolks, then stir them into the cheese sauce with the chives. Season well with pepper, and add a little salt if necessary.
6 Beat the egg whites until stiff but not dry. Fold them into the cheese mixture with a large metal spoon, in a figure-of-eight motion, using the edges of the spoon to cut through the mixture cleanly.
7 Pour the mixture into the prepared soufflé mold. Run a round-bladed knife through the mixture to make an attractive "crown" effect.
8 Bake in the oven for 50 minutes or until the soufflé is well risen and golden. When lightly shaken, it should only wobble slightly. Serve at once, straight from the dish.

Tasty cheese cakes

MAKES 8

1 cup coarsely shredded Red Leicester or Cheshire cheese

1 cup finely shredded sharp Cheddar cheese

2 tablespoons butter or margarine

1 small onion, minced

2½ cups soft wholewheat or white bread crumbs

½ teaspoon dried thyme

½ cup cottage cheese

salt and freshly ground black pepper

2 eggs, beaten

1 teaspoon water

2 tablespoons chopped fresh parsley

vegetable oil, for frying

For garnish

8 small gherkins, halved or cut in fans

8 olives, stuffed with pimiento, halved

1 Melt the butter in a skillet. Add the onion and cook gently for 5 minutes until soft and lightly colored. Remove

Below: Egg and onion bake
Right: Curried eggs with rice

from the pan with a slotted spoon and cool on absorbent kitchen paper.

2 In a bowl, mix the shredded cheeses with 1½ cups of the bread crumbs, the thyme, cottage cheese, and salt and pepper to taste. Add two-thirds of the egg and mix well.

3 Divide the mixture into 8 and shape each portion into a flat round cake. Refrigerate for 30 minutes – this will help them to hold their shape while they are cooking.

4 Mix the remaining egg with 1 teaspoon of cold water in a shallow bowl. Mix the remaining bread crumbs with the parsley and salt and pepper; spread out on a flat plate.

5 Coat the cakes in the egg, then in the bread crumb mixture

6 Heat about ½ inch of oil in a skillet until it is hot enough to turn a dry bread cube golden in 50 seconds. Add the cakes to the pan and cook for 2-3 minutes on each side until just browned. Do not cook the cheese cakes longer than it takes to brown the outside or the cheese will melt too much. Drain them well on absorbent kitchen paper.

7 Serve at once, garnished with the gherkins and olive halves.

Egg and onion bake

SERVES 4

4 eggs

2 large onions, finely chopped

salt and freshly ground black pepper

2½ cups hot milk

¾ cup shredded Cheddar cheese

1 tablespoon margarine or butter

1 tablespoon sunflower or vegetable oil

2 tablespoons finely chopped fresh chervil or parsley

margarine, for greasing

Cheese Sauce

2 tablespoons margarine or butter

¼ cup wholewheat or all-purpose flour

2½ cups milk

1 cup finely shredded Cheddar cheese

1 teaspoon Dijon mustard

1 Preheat the oven to 300°F and lightly grease a 5-cup ovenproof dish with margarine.

2 Put the eggs in a bowl and season with salt and pepper. Beat the eggs, then beat in the milk and cheese and pour into the prepared dish. Half-fill a roasting pan with boiling water and

place the dish in the pan. Bake in the oven for 1½ hours or until the mixture is firm.

3 About 15 minutes before the end of the cooking time, melt the butter with the oil in a skillet. Add the onions and cook gently for 5 minutes until soft and lightly colored. Stir in the chervil, remove from the heat and set aside.

4 Preheat the broiler to high.

5 Meanwhile, make the sauce: Melt the butter in a small saucepan, sprinkle in the flour and stir over low heat for 1-2 minutes until straw-colored. Off heat, gradually stir in the milk. Return to the heat and simmer, stirring, until the sauce is thick and smooth. Stir in half the shredded cheese and the mustard. Season to taste with salt and pepper.

6 When the egg mixture is cooked, spoon the fried onion mixture evenly over the top.

7 Spoon the cheese sauce over the layer of onions and sprinkle with the remaining cheese.

8 Place the dish under the broiler until the cheese has melted and is golden brown and bubbling. Serve the egg and onion bake at once, straight from the dish.

Curried eggs with biriani rice

SERVES 4

8 eggs
2 tablespoons vegetable oil
1 onion, finely chopped
1 clove garlic, minced
1 tablespoon ground cumin or coriander
1 teaspoon ground turmeric
½ teaspoon chili powder or to taste
salt
4 large tomatoes, peeled and chopped
2½ cups vegetable stock
freshly ground black pepper

Biriani rice

1⅓ cups Basmati, Patna or long-grain rice, rinsed and drained
2 tablespoon vegetable oil
1 teaspoon ground cumin
½ teaspoon ground turmeric
3 cups vegetable stock
1½ cups frozen mixed vegetables
2 tablespoons softened butter

1 Cook the eggs in boiling water for 8 minutes until just hard-cooked. Drain and reserve.

2 Heat the oil in a large heavy-bottomed pan or Dutch oven, add the onion, garlic, spices and salt to taste and cook gently for 5 minutes until the onion is soft, stirring constantly.

3 Add the chopped tomatoes to the pan and stir-fry for a few minutes. Stir in the stock and bring to a boil. Lower the heat and simmer uncovered for 20 minutes, stirring occasionally.

4 Make the biriani rice: Heat the oil in a heavy pan, add the rice, spices and salt to taste and cook gently for 5 minutes, stirring constantly.

5 Pour in the second quantity of stock and the frozen mixed vegetables, stir once, then cover and cook over gentle heat for 20 minutes until the rice is tender.

6 Shell the hard-cooked eggs and add to the curry sauce. Cook gently for a further 20 minutes, spooning the sauce over the eggs from time to time so they become well-coated.

7 When the rice is tender, fork in the softened butter and add salt and pepper to taste. Arrange the rice around the edge of a warmed serving dish.

8 Taste and adjust the seasoning of the sauce. Spoon the eggs into the center of the rice, then pour the curry sauce over the top. Serve at once.

Lentil lasagne

SERVES 4-6

1 cup split red lentils
2 tablespoons vegetable oil, plus 1 teaspoon
1 onion, chopped
2 cloves garlic, minced
1 small green pepper, seeded and chopped
1 can (16 oz) tomatoes
1 bay leaf
1¾ cup vegetable stock or water
⅔ cup red wine
2 tablespoons ketchup
pinch each of dried oregano, thyme and basil
salt and freshly ground black pepper
¼ lb dry wholewheat lasagne noodles
1½ quantity cheese sauce (page 62)
½ cup shredded Cheddar cheese

1 Preheat the oven to 400°F.
2 Heat 2 tablespoons oil in a sauce-pan, add the onion and sauté gently for 10 minutes. Add the garlic, lentils, pepper, tomatoes, bay leaf, stock and wine. Bring to a boil, lower the heat and simmer for 20-30 minutes, until the lentils are tender. Remove the bay leaf, add the ketchup and herbs, and season to taste with salt and pepper.
3 Meanwhile, cook the lasagne in a very large pan of salted water, with 1 teaspoon oil added to it, for about 12 minutes or until just tender. Drain, rinse under cold running water, then leave to drain on absorbent kitchen paper.
4 Put a layer of the lentil mixture into a shallow ovenproof dish and cover with some pieces of lasagne; follow this with another layer of the lentil mixture, then more lasagne and any remaining lentil mixture. Pour the cheese sauce over the top and sprinkle with the shredded cheese.
5 Bake in the oven for about 45 minutes, until golden brown.

Tagliatelle in parsley sauce

SERVES 4

¾ lb fresh or dry tagliatelle
1 tablespoon vegetable oil
grated Parmesan cheese, to serve

Sauce

3 cups fresh parsley sprigs
2 large cloves garlic, chopped
¼ cup pine kernels (pignoli)
⅔ cup olive oil
salt
½ cup grated Parmesan cheese
freshly ground black pepper

1 First make the sauce: Put the parsley, garlic, pine kernels and oil into a blender. Add a pinch of salt and purée for 1 minute until smooth.
2 Add the ½ cup grated Parmesan cheese and purée for 1 minute more, then season with freshly ground black pepper to taste.
3 Bring a large saucepan of salted water to a boil. Add the oil and fresh tagliatelle and stir once. Bring back to a boil and cook for 2-3 minutes until tender, yet firm to the bite. (Cook dry tagliatelle for 5-6 minutes or according to package directions, until tender.)
4 Drain the tagliatelle well, then spoon into a warmed serving dish. Stir

Below: Tagliatelle in parsley sauce
Right: Creamy rigatoni

the sauce and add to the dish. Quickly toss the tagliatelle with 2 forks to mix it with the sauce.

5 Serve at once while still hot, with a bowl filled with grated Parmesan cheese passed separately.

Creamy rigatoni

SERVES 4

¾ lb dry rigatoni or 3 cups short-cut macaroni
salt
1 tablespoon vegetable oil
½ cup plus 2 tablespoons butter
1 cup sliced button mushrooms
⅔ cup light cream
2 egg yolks
¾ cup grated Parmesan cheese
pinch of freshly grated nutmeg
freshly ground black pepper
⅔ cup frozen peas, cooked
½ cup grated Parmesan cheese

1 Bring a large saucepan of salted water to a boil. Add the rigatoni and oil, lower the heat and simmer for about 12 minutes until rigatoni is tender, yet firm to the bite.

2 Meanwhile, melt 2 tablespoons butter in a skillet. Add the mushrooms and sauté over moderate heat until just tender. Set aside.

3 Make the sauce: Melt the remaining butter in a large saucepan. Remove from the heat and set aside. In a bowl, quickly mix the cream, egg yolks and Parmesan with the nutmeg. Season with salt and plenty of pepper. Add this mixture to the melted butter in the pan and stir well.

4 When the rigatoni is nearly cooked, set the saucepan with the sauce mixture over very low heat to warm it through slightly; make sure that the eggs do not scramble.

5 Drain the cooked rigatoni, add to the cream sauce with the peas and the mushrooms. Stir continuously for a few seconds, then pile into warmed individual serving dishes, sprinkle each portion with Parmesan and serve at once.

Pasta with tomatoes

SERVES 4

¾ lb dry wholewheat spaghetti
grated Parmesan cheese, to serve

Sauce

1½ lb tomatoes, peeled and roughly chopped
2 tablespoons butter
2 tablespoons olive or vegetable oil
2 onions, roughly chopped
1 clove garlic, minced
1 cup vegetable stock
½ cup dried currants
2 teaspoons wine vinegar
1 teaspoon sugar
1 bay leaf
½ teaspoon dried basil
½ teaspoon dried thyme
½ teaspoon ground cinnamon
salt and freshly ground black pepper

1 Make the sauce: Heat the butter and oil in a large saucepan, add the onions and garlic and cook gently for 5 minutes until the onions are soft and lightly colored.

2 Add the tomatoes, stock, currants, vinegar, sugar, herbs and cinnamon. Season with salt and pepper. Bring to a boil, then lower the heat and simmer, uncovered, for 40-50 minutes, until thick, stirring occasionally and breaking up the tomato pieces with a wooden spoon.

3 Meanwhile bring a large pan of salted water to a boil. Add the spaghetti, bring back to a boil and cook for 15-20 minutes or until tender, yet firm to the bite. Drain the spaghetti thoroughly in a colander.

4 Divide the spaghetti among 4 warmed individual serving plates or shallow soup bowls and top each with a ladleful of the hot sauce. Serve the spaghetti at once, with plenty of grated Parmesan cheese passed separately in a small bowl.

Eggplant pasta bake

SERVES 4

1 large eggplant
salt
¼ cup olive oil
1 clove garlic, minced (optional)
1 onion, chopped
1 green pepper, seeded and finely chopped
2 cans (16 oz size) tomatoes, chopped
6 tablespoons red wine
2 teaspoons tomato paste
½ teaspoon sugar
1 tablespoon finely chopped fresh basil or
* 1 teaspoon dried basil*
freshly ground black pepper
6 oz dried tagliatelle
12 slices processed cheese
¼ cup grated Parmesan cheese
vegetable oil, for greasing
coriander sprigs, for garnish (optional)

1 Wipe the eggplant with a damp cloth and trim off the stem. Slice the eggplant in ¼ inch thick slices and put them in a colander in layers, sprinkling salt between each layer. Cover with a plate and place a heavy weight on top. Leave for about 1 hour to draw out the bitter juices then rinse the slices and pat dry on absorbent kitchen paper.

2 Preheat the oven to 350°F.

3 Heat 1 tablespoon of the oil in a saucepan, add the garlic, if using, the onion and green pepper and cook gently for about 5 minutes until the onion is soft and lightly colored. Stir in tomatoes with juices, wine and tomato paste. Bring to a boil, stir in the sugar and basil and season with salt and pepper to taste. Let the sauce boil gently for about 30-40 minutes to reduce and thicken.

4 Meanwhile, bring a pan of salted water to a boil and add 1 teaspoon of oil. Cook the tagliatelle for 5-6 minutes until it is just tender, then drain thoroughly.

5 Heat the remaining oil in a skillet, add the eggplant slices and cook gently until they are lightly colored on both sides. Remove with a slotted spoon and drain well on absorbent kitchen paper.

6 Grease a 7 × 11 inch ovenproof dish with melted butter and spread a third of the tomato sauce over the base. Put half the tagliatelle on top, followed by half the eggplant slices and half the processed cheese. Cover with another third of the tomato sauce and then the remaining tagliatelle, eggplant slices and processed cheese. Spread the remaining tomato sauce over the cheese slices and sprinkle the Parmesan cheese on top.

7 Cook the pasta bake in the oven for about 20 minutes, until heated through.

8 Garnish with coriander sprigs, if liked, and serve immediately, straight from the dish.

Vegetable lasagne

SERVES 4

7 oz pre-cooked lasagne noodles
2 tablespoons vegetable oil
1 onion, finely chopped
1 cup sliced button mushrooms
1 package (10 oz) frozen spinach, thawed and
* well drained*
1-2 tablespoons lemon juice
¼ teaspoon freshly grated nutmeg
salt and freshly ground black pepper
1 cup cottage cheese
1 cup finely shredded sharp Cheddar
* cheese*
1 can (10 oz) artichoke hearts, drained and
* finely chopped*
margarine, for greasing

Sauce

2 tablespoons butter or margarine
2 tablespoons wholewheat or all-purpose flour
1 cup milk
4-5 tablespoons grated Parmesan cheese

1 Preheat the oven to 375°F. Grease an 8 inch square shallow ovenproof dish.

2 Heat the oil in a heavy-bottomed pan and sauté the onion for 3-4 minutes, until soft but not colored. Add the mushrooms and cook, stirring, for 5 minutes. Add the spinach, lemon

juice and nutmeg and season with salt and pepper. Simmer for 5-6 minutes, stirring occasionally.

3   Meanwhile, mix the cottage cheese with the shredded Cheddar in a bowl; season to taste with pepper.

4   Make the sauce: Melt butter in a small pan, sprinkle in the flour and stir over a low heat for 1-2 minutes, until straw-colored. Remove from heat and gradually stir in the milk. Return to the heat and simmer, stirring, until thick and smooth. Add the Parmesan cheese and salt and pepper to taste.

5   Put one-third of the lasagne in the prepared dish, spread with half the cottage cheese mixture, then the spinach mixture. Top with another third of lasagne, spread with the remaining cottage cheese mixture, then the artichoke hearts. Cover with all the remaining lasagne and spread sauce on top.

6   Bake in oven for 30-35 minutes, until the top is bubbling and golden. Let cool slightly before serving.

Spaghetti with zucchini sauce

SERVES 4

3/4 lb dry wholewheat spaghetti

1 lb zucchini, trimmed and cut in
*   1/4 inch slices*

2 tablespoons vegetable oil

1/4 cup butter

1 onion, finely chopped

1 clove garlic, finely chopped

1 green pepper, seeded and thinly sliced

3/4 lb tomatoes, peeled, seeded and sliced

1 teaspoon dried oregano

salt and freshly ground black pepper

grated Parmesan cheese, to serve

1   Make the sauce: Heat the oil and 2 tablespoons butter in a skillet, add the onion and sauté gently for 5 minutes until soft and lightly colored. Add the garlic, green pepper and zucchini, stir well and sauté over moderate heat for 2 minutes. Cover the pan, lower the heat and simmer for 10 minutes, stirring occasionally.

2   Add the tomatoes and oregano, with the salt and pepper to taste, and cook, uncovered, over moderate heat for a further 10 minutes. Taste the zucchini sauce and adjust the seasoning if necessary.

3   Meanwhile, cook the spaghetti in a large pan of boiling, salted water for 15-20 minutes, or until just tender.

4   Drain the spaghetti and toss it with the remaining butter in a warmed serving dish. Top with the sauce and serve hot, with the cheese passed separately.

Pasta kugel

SERVES 4

2 cups dry wholewheat pasta rings

3 eggs

1 cup small curd cottage cheese

2/3 cup sour cream

2 tablespoons brown sugar

2/3 cup seedless raisins

1/4 teaspoon salt

1/4 teaspoon ground cinnamon

1/4 teaspoon freshly grated nutmeg

margarine, for greasing

fresh peaches, to serve

Topping

2 tablespoons chopped mixed nuts

1/4 teaspoon ground cinnamon

1 tablespoon butter

1   Preheat the oven to 350°F. Grease a 5-cup ovenproof dish generously with margarine.

Left: Eggplant pasta bake
Above: Spaghetti with zucchini sauce

2   Bring a pan of salted water to a boil and cook the pasta rings for 12 minutes or according to package directions until they are tender, but still firm to the bite.

3   Meanwhile, beat the eggs in a bowl, add the small curd cottage cheese, sour cream and sugar and beat with a fork until smooth. Mix in the raisins, salt and spices.

4   Drain the cooked pasta rings and return them to the rinsed-out pan. Pour the curd cheese mixture over the pasta and stir it until evenly coated. Transfer the mixture to the prepared dish, sprinkle with nuts and cinnamon and dot the surface with the butter.

5   Bake in the oven, uncovered, for about 30 minutes, until the top is golden and filling has set around the edge but is still creamy in the middle. Serve the pasta kugel at once, straight from the dish accompanied by fresh, sliced peaches.

● *Kugel* is the Jewish name for pudding, usually made of noodles or potatoes and baked. Although many kugels, like this one, are semisweet, they are generally served as a savory dish.

Salads

*You'll find a salad for every occasion in this chapter –
add color and texture to a meal with a crunchy side salad, or keep
healthy with a substantial salad for lunch or supper.*

Gado-gado

SERVES 4
1 potato, scrubbed but unpeeled
*1½ cups shredded green cabbage or collard
    greens*
½ cup sliced green beans
⅔ cup thinly sliced carrots
½ cauliflower, divided into flowerets
1 bunch of watercress, divided into sprigs
2 cups beansprouts
Sauce
*½ cup shelled raw (not roasted or salted)
    peanuts*
vegetable oil, for frying
1 clove garlic, minced
2 shallots or ½ small onion, minced
salt
½ teaspoon chili powder
½ teaspoon light brown sugar
1½ cups water
juice of 1 lemon
For garnish
1 large egg, hard-cooked and cut in wedges
1 lettuce, shredded
¼ cucumber, sliced
*1 onion, sliced in rings and sautéed until crisp
    and brown*
crackers or potato chips, broken up

1 Make the sauce: Heat enough oil in a large, heavy skillet or wok to cover the peanuts. Add the peanuts and sauté over moderate heat for 5-6 minutes, stirring occasionally. Remove the peanuts with a slotted spoon and drain on absorbent kitchen paper. Let cool. Pour all but 1 teaspoon of the oil out of the pan.
2 Grind the cooled peanuts to a fine powder in a food processor or coffee grinder, or pound them to a fine powder, using a pestle and mortar.
3 Reheat the oil in the pan, add the garlic and shallots, season with salt and sauté for 1 minute. Stir in the chili powder and sugar and add the water. Bring the mixture to a boil, then stir in the ground peanuts. Lower the heat and simmer, stirring occasionally, for 4-6 minutes until the sauce thickens. Set aside.
4 Bring 3 saucepans of salted water to a boil. Add the potato to one pan and boil gently for 15 minutes.
5 Meanwhile, add the cabbage, green beans, carrots and cauliflower to another pan and boil gently for 4 minutes.
6 Add the watercress and the beansprouts to the third pan and boil gently for 2-3 minutes.
7 Drain all the vegetables very thoroughly. Let the potato cool slightly, then cut in thin slices.
8 Pile the warm cabbage, green beans, carrots, cauliflower, watercress and beansprouts onto a round serving dish. Arrange the potato slices and hard-cooked egg wedges on top, and arrange the shredded lettuce and sliced cucumber around the edge.
9 Stir the lemon juice into the sauce in the pan and heat through gently. Pour the sauce over the salad. Garnish with fried onion rings and broken-up crackers. Serve at once.

● This popular Indonesian salad is best served with the vegetables still just warm. Peanuts feature prominently in Indonesian cooking, and Gado-gado – which means "a mixture" – is topped with a nutty sauce. Make sure that you buy raw peanuts; roasted or salted ones will not give the right flavor or texture.

Bulgur wheat and parsley salad

SERVES 4
2 cups bulgur wheat
5 cups warm water
3 cups chopped fresh parsley
4 scallions, minced
6 tablespoons olive oil
juice of 1 lemon
1 clove garlic, minced
salt and freshly ground black pepper
½ lb tomatoes, cut in wedges
4 thin lemon slices, for garnish

1 Put the bulgur wheat into a large bowl. Pour in the water and let soak for 45 minutes. Drain the wheat in a strainer and using your hands, squeeze out as much water as possible. Put the drained wheat into a large bowl.
2 Mix the chopped parsley and scallions into the wheat.
3 Beat together the oil, lemon juice, garlic and plenty of salt and pepper. Fold the dressing into the wheat and parsley mixture.
4 Pile the salad onto a flat serving dish, building it up into a pyramid. Arrange the tomato wedges around the edge of the dish.
5 To make lemon twists for garnish: Make a cut from the outside of one lemon slice to the center, then twist one half of the slice backward. Repeat with remaining slices. Place the lemon twists on top of the salad. Serve at room temperature.

*Gado-gado, an attractive salad made
from lightly cooked vegetables*

Chick-pea salad

SERVES 4

½ cup chick-peas
3 tablespoons olive oil
1 tablespoon wine vinegar
salt and freshly ground black pepper
1 lb tomatoes, peeled and sliced
1 onion, thinly sliced
2 teaspoons chopped fresh basil, or 1 teaspoon dried basil

1 Put the chick-peas into a deep bowl, cover with plenty of cold water and let soak for 8 hours.
2 Drain the chick-peas, rinse under cold running water, then put them into a saucepan and cover with fresh cold water. Bring to a boil, then lower heat and simmer for about 1 hour until tender. Add more water during cooking if necessary.
3 Drain the cooked chick-peas and let cool.
4 Put the oil and vinegar into a bowl. Mix together with a fork, and season to taste with salt and pepper. Add the chick-peas and mix gently until well coated with dressing. Take care not to break them up.
5 Lay the tomato and onion slices in a shallow serving dish and sprinkle with the basil and salt and pepper to taste. Spoon the dressed chick-peas over the top. Serve cold.

Brown rice salad

SERVES 4

⅔ cup brown rice
salt
1 sweet red pepper, seeded and diced
1 green pepper, seeded and diced
2 tablespoons butter or margarine
1 Bermuda onion, chopped
½ lb tomatoes, peeled, seeded and chopped
½ small cucumber, diced
halved stuffed olives and bunch of watercress, for garnish

Dressing

3 tablespoons vegetable oil
1 teaspoon wine vinegar or lemon juice
pinch of dry mustard
pinch of superfine sugar
salt and freshly ground black pepper

1 Rinse the rice and put it into a large saucepan of boiling salted water. Bring to a boil again, lower heat and simmer, very gently, for about 40 minutes, until the rice is cooked and has absorbed all the water. If necessary, add more boiling water during cooking. Rinse under cold running water and let stand in a strainer to drain thoroughly.
2 Meanwhile, soften the diced peppers slightly by plunging them into boiling water for 30 seconds. Drain and refresh immediately under cold running water.
3 Melt the butter in a skillet, add the onion and cook over gentle heat for 5 minutes until it is soft and translucent. Off heat, stir in the peppers, tomatoes and cucumber.
4 Put the ingredients for the dressing in a large bowl and beat with a fork to blend thoroughly.
5 Add the drained rice to the dressing with the vegetables and gently mix all the ingredients together, using 2 forks. Pack into a 4-cup plain ring mold and refrigerate for at least 1 hour.
6 To unmold: Run a knife around the ring mold. Invert a serving platter on top and give the mold a sharp tap. Fill the center of the ring with watercress and surround with halved olives. Serve at once.

Stuffed cucumber salad

SERVES 4

1 large cucumber, cut in 24 even slices
1 head Boston lettuce, leaves separated
2 cups finely shredded carrots
3 tablespoons golden raisins
small parsley sprigs and a few chopped walnuts, for garnish

Filling

1 cup small curd cottage cheese
3/4 cup chopped walnuts
2 teaspoons finely chopped fresh parsley
2 teaspoons chopped fresh chives or minced scallion
1/2 teaspoon mild paprika
salt and freshly ground black pepper

Dressing

5 tablespoons vegetable oil
2 tablespoons distilled white vinegar
large pinch of dry mustard
pinch of superfine sugar

1 Make the filling: Put all the filling ingredients in a bowl, season with salt and pepper and mix well.
2 Remove the seeds from each slice of cucumber with an apple corer or a small sharp knife. Season with salt and pepper and set out on a flat platter.
3 Divide the filling among the cucumber slices, pressing it into the central hole and piling it up on top.
4 Make the dressing: Put all the dressing ingredients in a screw-top jar, season with salt and pepper, then shake the jar well to mix.
5 Arrange the lettuce leaves on 4 individual plates and drizzle a teaspoonful of the dressing over each serving. Transfer 6 cucumber slices to each plate, arranging them in a ring.
6 Mix the shredded carrots with the golden raisins in a bowl and add the remaining dressing. Toss to coat thoroughly, then pile into the center of the rings of stuffed cucumber slices. Garnish 3 cucumber slices on each plate with a parsley sprig and 3 slices with a few chopped walnuts. Serve at once.

Left: Brown rice salad
Right: Gazpacho salad

Gazpacho salad

SERVES 4

1 sweet red pepper, seeded and thinly sliced
1 green pepper, seeded and thinly sliced
1/2 large cucumber, pared and thinly sliced
3/4 lb tomatoes, peeled and thinly sliced
sugar, for sprinkling
1 onion, thinly sliced
salt and freshly ground black pepper
10 tablespoons soft white or wholewheat bread crumbs

French dressing

6 tablespoons olive oil
2 tablespoons lemon juice
1 clove garlic, minced

To serve

10 ripe olives
1 tablespoon chopped fresh parsley or finely chopped chervil

1 Plunge the peppers in boiling water for 30 seconds, and then immerse them immediately in cold water.
2 Make the French dressing: Put all the ingredients in a screw-top jar, season with salt and pepper, then shake the jar well to mix well.
3 In a glass bowl, put a layer of cucumber, followed by a layer of tomatoes and a sprinkling of sugar, a layer of onion and a layer of mixed red and green peppers. Season with salt and pepper and sprinkle over 2 tablespoons bread crumbs and 2 tablespoons French dressing.
4 Continue these layers, finishing with a layer of 4 tablespoons breadcrumbs. Cover these with French dressing so that they are well soaked, then cover the bowl with plastic wrap and refrigerate for 2-3 hours.
5 Just before serving, sprinkle with olives and chopped parsley.

Wheaty pea and vegetable salad

SERVES 4

1 cup wholewheat grains or cracked wheat

½ cup green or yellow split peas

2 tablespoons olive oil

1 tablespoon red wine vinegar

salt and freshly ground black pepper

2 carrots, shredded

2 celery stalks, chopped

2 inch piece of cucumber, pared and chopped

4 scallions, chopped

2 tomatoes, peeled and chopped

4 lettuce leaves, shredded

2 tablespoons raisins

a little garden cress, for garnish

Dressing

¾ cup small curd cottage cheese

¼ cup milk

1 tablespoon thick bottled mayonnaise

1 Put the wholewheat grains in a bowl, cover with cold water and let soak for 8 hours or overnight.

2 Next day, cook the wholewheat grains in a pressure cooker for 25 minutes, or simmer in plenty of water for 1¼ – 1½ hours, or until the grains are tender and beginning to burst. Drain and let cool slightly.

3 Meanwhile, put the split peas in a saucepan of cold water and simmer for about 25 minutes, until just tender but still whole.

4 Put the oil and vinegar into a large bowl and mix together. Season with salt and pepper to taste, then add the wheat and peas. Let the mixture cool completely.

5 Stir in the carrots, celery, cucumber, scallions, tomatoes, lettuce and raisins, tossing gently until well coated with the oil and vinegar mixture. Divide the salad among 4 individual bowls.

6 Make the dressing: Beat together the small curd cottage cheese, milk and mayonnaise until smooth.

7 Put a large spoonful of dressing on top of each bowl of salad and sprinkle with garden cress. Serve at once.

Two-bean salad

SERVES 4

⅓ cup dried red kidney beans, soaked overnight

½ cup dried navy beans, soaked overnight

1 small onion, chopped

1 bay leaf

2 large celery stalks, thinly sliced

1 green pepper, seeded and diced

Dressing

6 tablespoons olive oil

2 tablespoons wine vinegar

1 clove garlic, minced

salt and freshly ground black pepper

1 Drain the soaked kidney beans and navy beans, then transfer to a saucepan, cover with water and bring to a boil. Boil vigorously for 10 minutes, then drain and cover with fresh water.

2 Add the onion and bay leaf and bring back to a boil. Lower the heat slightly, half cover with a lid and simmer for about 1 hour until the beans are tender.

3 Meanwhile, make the dressing: Put the ingredients in a screw-top jar, with salt and pepper to taste. Replace the lid firmly and shake well to mix the dressing.

4 Drain the beans and discard the cooking liquid and bay leaf. Transfer to a serving dish and pour over the dressing, while the beans are still warm. Mix well and let stand for at least 1 hour or overnight.

5 Add the celery and diced pepper to the beans, taste and adjust seasoning, if necessary, and stir to mix well. Serve at once.

White cabbage salad

SERVES 6

1 lb white cabbage
½ cucumber
6 scallions
3 hard-cooked eggs, for garnish

Dressing

⅓ cup vegetable oil
2 tablespoons white wine or tarragon vinegar
2 tablespoons chopped fresh mint
¼ teaspoon Dijon mustard
salt and freshly ground black pepper

1 Remove the coarse stem of the cabbage. Using a sharp knife or the shredding plate of a food processor, finely shred the cabbage and put it into a salad bowl.

2 Cut the cucumber in small dice about ¼ inch square and add to the cabbage.

3 Thinly slice the scallions and add to the salad.

4 Make the dressing: Put the ingredients in a screw-top jar, with salt and pepper to taste. Replace the lid firmly and shake well to mix.

5 Cut the hard-cooked eggs in thin slices. Place the egg slices around the edge of the cabbage and cucumber salad. Pour over the dressing, toss until the salad is thoroughly coated and serve at once.

Above left: Two-bean salad makes a substantial side dish
Right: Serve White cabbage salad with cucumber for a light lunch

Sweet pepper salad

SERVES 6

4 peppers
1 Bermuda onion, finely sliced
¼ cup olive oil
2 tablespoons distilled white vinegar
salt

1 Preheat the broiler to high.
2 Wash the peppers and pat dry thoroughly with absorbent kitchen paper. Place the peppers on the broiler rack and broil them, turning them often with kitchen tongs until the skins are charred black on all sides.

3 Immediately transfer the peppers to a large bowl and cover closely with several layers of absorbent kitchen paper to seal in the heat and allow the peppers to cook through. Cover the bowl tightly with a clean cloth; leave at room temperature for at least 24 hours.
4 The next day, remove the skins: One at a time, hold the peppers under cold running water and rub off the skins with your fingers. Gently squeezing the base of each pepper, pull out the core and the seeds in one piece. Discard the cores and seeds. Rinse peppers under cold running water.
5 Tear peppers into long strips with your fingers and arrange on a serving

dish with the finely sliced onion.
6 Put the oil in a small bowl with the vinegar and salt to taste. Mix well with a fork, then pour over the peppers. Serve as soon as possible, at room temperature.

Beet and orange salad

SERVES 4

4 cooked beet, peeled and sliced
2 oranges
1 head lettuce, leaves separated
2 large tomatoes, sliced
3-4 teaspoons chopped walnuts
Dressing
1 teaspoon minced onion
1 teaspoon chopped chives
good pinch of salt
½ teaspoon prepared English mustard
good pinch of superfine sugar
freshly ground black pepper
3 tablespoons olive or vegetable oil
1 tablespoon wine vinegar
dash of soy sauce.

1 Peel the oranges over a bowl to catch the juices; reserve juice. Slice oranges.
2 Line a salad platter with lettuce. Arrange the orange and beet slices alternately in a ring on top of the lettuce. Arrange overlapping slices of tomato in the center of the dish and sprinkle with walnuts.
3 Make the dressing: Put all the ingredients in a screw-top jar with the reserved orange juice. Shake to mix well.
4 Spoon the dressing over the salad and serve at once.

Tangy potato salad

SERVES 6

1 lb potatoes, cut in even-size chunks
salt
¾ cup thick bottled mayonnaise, heavy cream or sour cream
1 tablespoon olive oil
1 tablespoon grated fresh horseradish or creamy horseradish sauce
freshly ground black pepper
½ teaspoon mild paprika
1 teaspoon chopped fresh parsley

1 Put the potato chunks in a large saucepan; cover with cold water, add a pinch of salt and bring to a boil. Lower the heat slightly and simmer for 20-25 minutes until the potatoes are tender.

2 Meanwhile, put the mayonnaise into a large serving bowl and stir in the olive oil, horseradish and salt and pepper to taste.

3 Drain the potatoes and let cool slightly for about 10 minutes.

4 Add the potatoes to the mayonnaise, carefully turning them to ensure that all the pieces are evenly coated. Let potato salad stand for 1 hour.

5 Just before serving, sprinkle the paprika and chopped parsley over the top of the salad.

Watercress salad with curry dressing

SERVES 6

4 bunches of watercress, weighing about
*   1 lb in total*

2 oranges

Dressing

6-8 tablespoons olive oil

2 tablespoons wine vinegar

1 tablespoon lemon juice

1 tablespoon curry powder

coarse salt and freshly ground black pepper

1 Rinse the watercress gently and remove the thick stem ends and any damaged or yellowed leaves. Drain well, then pat dry. Refrigerate for at least 1 hour.

2 Peel the oranges with a sharp, serrated knife; trim away the pith. Cut between the sections and the membranes to remove the orange sections. Remove any seeds from the sections. Set aside.

3 Make the dressing: Put all the ingredients in a bowl with salt and pepper to taste. Beat well to mix. Refrigerate until ready to assemble the salad.

4 To serve: Place the watercress in a salad bowl and arrange the orange sections on top. Stir the dressing and pour over the salad. Toss the salad at the table, until each leaf of watercress is glistening with dressing.

Left: Sweet pepper salad
Right: Greek-style mushrooms

Greek-style mushrooms

SERVES 4

4 cups small button mushrooms

⅓ cup olive oil

1 onion, minced

6 tablespoons water

juice of ½ lemon

1 clove garlic, minced

½ teaspoon dried thyme

2 bay leaves

½ lb tomatoes, peeled, seeded and chopped

2 tablespoons chopped fresh parsley

salt and freshly ground black pepper

1 Heat half the oil in a saucepan, add the onion and cook over moderate heat for about 5 minutes, until soft and lightly colored.

2 Add the water, lemon juice, garlic, thyme, bay leaves, tomatoes and half the parsley. Season with salt and pepper to taste. Bring to a boil, then lower the heat and simmer very gently for 3-4 minutes, stirring occasionally.

3 Add the mushrooms to the tomato sauce and simmer gently, uncovered, for 15 minutes.

4 Remove from the heat and discard the bay leaves.

5 Transfer the mixture to a serving dish. (If the sauce is too thin, transfer the mushrooms to a serving dish with a slotted spoon and boil the sauce for a few minutes to reduce.)

6 Garnish with remaining parsley and serve warm, cold or chilled.

Avocado and grapefruit salad

SERVES 4

2 small avocados
1 small grapefruit
2 eating apples
1 small head lettuce, leaves separated

Dressing

1 tablespoon honey
2 tablespoons cider vinegar
6 tablespoons olive oil
salt and freshly ground black pepper

1 To make the dressing: Mix together the honey, vinegar and olive oil in a bowl. Beat with a fork and season to taste.
2 Peel the grapefruit. Hold it over a bowl to catch the juice and, using a small, sharp knife, trim away any white pith. Divide the grapefruit into sections and stir into the dressing.
3 Just before serving, halve the avocados lengthwise, then remove the seeds and peel. Slice the flesh and add immediately to the dressing. Toss.
4 Quarter, core and slice the apples. Toss them in the dressing. Taste and adjust seasoning. Arrange the lettuce leaves in a salad bowl, pile the salad in the center and serve at once.

Cucumber and strawberry salad

SERVES 4

¹/₂ cucumber, pared and thinly sliced
¹/₃ pint strawberries, sliced lengthwise
salt
sprigs of fennel leaves, for garnish

Above: Avocado and grapefruit salad
Right: Oriental citrus salad

Dressing

1 tablespoon olive oil
1 tablespoon distilled white vinegar
1 teaspoon sugar
freshly ground black pepper

1 Spread the cucumber out on a plate, sprinkle with salt and let stand for 30 minutes to draw out excess moisture. Drain and pat dry.
2 Make the dressing: Put all the dressing ingredients in a screw-top jar with salt and pepper. Shake to mix.
3 Arrange alternate circles of cucumber and strawberries on a flat, round serving platter.
4 Spoon the dressing over the salad, garnish with sprigs of fennel leaves and serve the salad at once.

Plum salad

SERVES 4

6 oz dessert plums
1/4 cucumber, cut in matchsticks
1 head Boston lettuce, shredded
6 scallions, finely chopped
4 sage leaves, chopped
1 tablespoon chopped fresh tarragon
1 tablespoon chopped fresh parsley
1/4 cup olive oil
2 tablespoons distilled white vinegar
salt and freshly ground black pepper

1 Halve and pit the plums and cut them lengthwise in thin slices.
2 Put the plum and cucumber slices, lettuce and scallions in a salad bowl and mix in the herbs. Beat the oil with the vinegar, then season to taste with salt and pepper. Fold into the salad and serve at once.

Oriental citrus salad

SERVES 4

1 grapefruit
2 oranges
1/2 cucumber, sliced
1 onion, sliced in rings
1 can (8 oz) water chestnuts, drained and sliced
1/4 lb fresh spinach, washed and thoroughly dried
1/4 lb Edam cheese, sliced
1 tablespoon distilled white vinegar
2 tablespoons sugar
2 teaspoons soy sauce
few drops of hot pepper sauce

1 Peel the grapefruit and oranges and divide into sections over a bowl to catch any juice. Put the fruit into a large bowl and mix in the cucumber, onion rings and the water chestnuts.
2 Arrange the spinach on a serving platter, then place the cheese in over-lapping slices at the edge.
3 Put the vinegar, sugar, soy sauce and hot pepper sauce into the bowl with the collected fruit juices and beat with a fork until well blended. Pour over the grapefruit mixture and toss.
4 Spoon the tossed salad onto the spinach. Refrigerate for 30 minutes, then serve at once.

Vegetable Accompaniments

With a little imagination, even the most familiar vegetables can be turned into exciting side dishes.

Chestnut sprouts

SERVES 4

1 lb small Brussels sprouts

salt

1/2 lb chestnuts

2/3 cup vegetable stock

1 celery stalk, halved

2 tablespoons butter

pinch of freshly grated nutmeg

freshly ground black pepper

1 Wash the sprouts, cut off the stem ends and remove any discolored leaves. Cut a cross in the stem end of each and let soak in a bowl of cold salted water.

2 Meanwhile, prepare the chestnuts: Nick each with a sharp knife, then place in a saucepan and cover with cold water. Gradually bring to a boil, lower heat and simmer for 10 minutes.

3 Remove the chestnuts from the heat, drain, then wrap in a thick folded dish towel to keep hot; the chestnuts must be kept hot to make peeling easier. Peel the chestnuts one at a time. Hold in a soft cloth or pot holder, insert a small sharp knife into the slit in the skin and prize off the outer and inner skins.

4 Place the peeled chestnuts in a saucepan, cover with stock and add the celery. Bring to a boil, then lower the heat and simmer gently for 30-40 minutes or until the peeled chestnuts are tender.

5 Meanwhile, bring a pan of salted water to a boil. Drain the sprouts and add to the pan. Cover and simmer for 8-10 minutes until just tender. The sprouts should be just tender but still firm; they will have a nice "nutty" texture and flavor. If overcooked they will be soft and will break up when combined with the chestnuts.

6 Drain the chestnuts and discard the celery. Drain the sprouts thoroughly, then return to the rinsed-out pan together with the chestnuts. Add the butter, nutmeg and salt and pepper to taste and toss to combine. Turn into a warmed serving dish and serve.

Sesame sprouts

SERVES 4

1/2 lb Brussels sprouts

salt and freshly ground black pepper

1/4 cup butter or margarine

1 onion, minced

1 clove garlic, minced (optional)

1/4 cup all-purpose flour

4 tablespoons tahini paste

1 vegetable bouillon cube, crumbled

1 1/2 cups orange juice

2/3 cup water

1 teaspoon honey

2 teaspoons sesame seeds and orange twists, for garnish

1 Wash and trim the Brussels sprouts, discarding any tough or discolored outer leaves. Cut a cross in stem end of each sprout.
2 Bring a pan of salted water to a boil and cook the Brussels sprouts for 8-10 minutes, until tender but still firm to the bite.
3 Meanwhile, make the sauce: Melt the butter in a small saucepan, add the onion and the garlic, if using, and sauté gently for 5 minutes until the onion is soft and lightly colored. Sprinkle in the flour and stir over low heat for 3 minutes. Add the tahini paste and crumbled bouillon cube and stir until smooth. Gradually stir in the orange juice and water, then simmer, stirring until thick and smooth. Stir in the honey and season to taste with salt and pepper.
4 Drain Brussels sprouts, transfer to a warmed serving dish and pour over the sauce. Sprinkle with sesame seeds, garnish with orange twists and serve at once.

Cauliflower Creole

SERVES 4

1 cauliflower
1 tablespoon vegetable oil
1 large onion, chopped
1 clove garlic, minced (optional)
1 can (16 oz) tomatoes
salt
2 tablespoons butter or margarine
1 large green or sweet red pepper, seeded and chopped
1/2-1 teaspoon hot pepper sauce
freshly ground black pepper

1 Heat the oil in a large saucepan, add the onion and garlic, if using, and gently sauté for 2-3 minutes until just tender.
2 Stir in the tomatoes, breaking them up against the side of the pan with a wooden spoon. Cover the saucepan and simmer gently for 20-30 minutes.
3 Meanwhile, bring a pan of salted water to a boil, plunge the cauliflower head down in it and cook for about 20 minutes until just tender. It is important not to overcook the cauliflower; it should be just tender.
4 Preheat the oven to 250°F. Drain the cauliflower well in a colander, then transfer to a warmed serving dish and keep hot in the oven.
5 Add the butter and green pepper to the tomato sauce, stir well and simmer for 5 minutes. Season to taste with hot pepper sauce, salt and freshly ground black pepper.
6 Pour a little of the sauce over the cauliflower, leaving some of the white flower showing. Pour the remaining sauce around the cauliflower. Serve at once.

Left: Chestnut sprouts
Below: Cauliflower Creole

Crunchy Provençal beans

SERVES 4

1 package (10 oz) frozen green beans
1 tablespoon vegetable oil
1 onion, chopped
1 large clove garlic, minced
1/2 lb tomatoes, peeled and chopped
1 teaspoon dried basil
salt and freshly ground black pepper
margarine, for greasing
tomato slices and sprigs of fresh parsley, for garnish

Topping

3/4 cup shredded Cheddar cheese
1 cup soft wholewheat bread crumbs

1 Preheat the oven to 425°F. Grease an ovenproof dish with margarine.
2 Heat the oil in a heavy-bottomed saucepan. Add the onion and garlic and sauté gently for 10 minutes until the onion is soft and lightly colored.
3 Add the tomatoes, with the basil and salt and pepper to taste, then simmer mixture over moderate heat, uncovered, for 10 minutes, stirring occasionally.
4 Meanwhile, cook the beans in boiling salted water for 8 minutes until they are just tender. Drain.
5 Stir the beans into the tomato mixture, then taste and adjust seasoning. Transfer to the greased dish.
6 Mix the shredded cheese with the bread crumbs and sprinkle evenly over the bean mixture. Place in the oven for 15-20 minutes until the top has browned. Serve at once, garnished with the tomato slices and sprigs of fresh parsley.

Below: Green bean special
Right: Orange potato croquettes

Green bean special

SERVES 4

1½ packages (10 oz size) frozen green beans
salt
chopped fresh parsley, for garnish

Sauce

3 egg yolks
1 tablespoon distilled white vinegar
small pinch of freshly grated nutmeg
1 teaspoon sugar (optional)
2 tablespoons heavy cream or sour cream
1 hard-cooked egg, finely chopped
freshly ground black pepper

1 Bring a large pan of salted water to a boil, add the beans and cook for 8 minutes or until the beans are just tender.

2 Meanwhile, make the sauce: Put the egg yolks, vinegar, nutmeg and sugar, if using, into a heatproof bowl then stand the bowl over a pan of gently simmering water – make sure that the bottom of the bowl does not touch the water or the eggs will cook too quickly. Beat over very low heat for about 6 minutes, or until the sauce is thick enough to coat the back of a spoon.

3 Remove the pan from the heat and immediately beat in the cream and chopped hard-cooked egg. Season the mixture to taste with salt and freshly ground black pepper.

4 Drain the beans and turn them onto a warmed serving plate. Pour over the sauce and garnish with chopped parsley. Serve at once.

Fava beans with garlic

SERVES 4-6

2 lb fresh Fava beans, unhulled weight
pinch of salt
2 tablespoons butter
1 clove garlic, minced
juice of ½ lemon
freshly ground black pepper
parsley sprigs, for garnish

1 Hull the beans, then put them in a saucepan and pour over enough water to just cover them. Add the salt, cover the pan and bring to a boil, then lower the heat slightly and simmer for about 5 minutes until just tender.

2 Meanwhile, melt the butter in a skillet, add the minced garlic and sauté gently for 2 minutes. Remove the pan from the heat.

3 Drain the beans and add to the garlic in the skillet. Stir over moderate heat for 1 minute, then season to taste with salt and pepper and turn into a warmed serving dish. Serve at once, garnished with parsley.

Orange potato croquettes

SERVES 4

1 lb potatoes, boiled and well drained
1 egg yolk
1 tablespoon butter or margarine
2 tablespoons hot milk
finely grated rind of 1 large orange
salt and freshly ground black pepper
orange slices, cut in twists, for garnish
vegetable oil, for deep-frying

Coating

1 egg, beaten
1½ cups fine dry wholewheat bread crumbs
⅓ cup all-purpose flour

1 Put the hot drained potatoes in a saucepan, place over low heat and shake the pan vigorously until the potatoes are completely dry. Turn into a bowl, then mash.

2 Stir the egg yolk, butter and hot milk into the mashed potato, beat until smooth. Beat in half the orange rind and season with salt and pepper to taste.

3 Divide the creamed potato into 16 portions. With floured hands, roll into cork shapes about 2 inches long.

4 Put the beaten egg and bread crumbs in separate shallow dishes. Stir the remaining orange rind into the bread crumbs. Roll potato croquettes in flour, then dip in beaten egg and roll in bread crumbs.

5 Heat the oil in a deep-fat fryer to 375°F or until a bread cube turns brown in 50 seconds. Lower the croquettes into the oil and fry for 4-5 minutes until golden brown. Remove with a slotted spoon and drain on absorbent kitchen paper. Serve hot, garnished with orange twists.

Scalloped potatoes

SERVES 4-6

1½ lb potatoes, thinly sliced
1 onion, chopped
1 cup shredded Cheddar cheese
salt and freshly ground black pepper
1 tablespoon butter or margarine
1 egg
1¼ cups milk
margarine, for greasing

1 Preheat the oven to 350°F. Grease a shallow ovenproof dish.
2 Arrange a layer of potato slices in the dish and sprinkle with a little of the onion and cheese. Season with salt and pepper. Continue making layers in this way, finishing with a layer of cheese. Dot the top with butter.
3 Beat the egg and milk together in a bowl and pour over the potatoes.
4 Cover the dish with foil and bake in the oven for 1½ hours, or until the potatoes are fork-tender all the way through. Serve at once.

Oven-baked new potatoes

SERVES 4

1½ lb small new potatoes, scrubbed
4 sprigs of mint
4 sprigs of parsley
salt and freshly ground black pepper
2 tablespoons butter or margarine
1 tablespoon chopped fresh mint or 1 teaspoon
*   dried mint*
1 tablespoon chopped fresh parsley

1 Preheat the oven to 350°F. Put the potatoes in a 6 cup ovenproof dish.
2 Tuck the mint and parsley sprigs among the potatoes and season to taste with salt and freshly ground black pepper. Dot the butter over the top of the potatoes.
3 Cover the dish and bake in the oven for 45-60 minutes until tender when pierced with a fine skewer. Using 2 spoons, turn the potatoes until evenly coated with the melted butter. Sprinkle with the chopped mint and parsley and serve at once.

Rösti

SERVES 4

1 lb potatoes, parboiled whole, cooled and
*   peeled*
1 large onion
salt and freshly ground black pepper
¼ cup butter

1 Shred the potatoes and onion, season generously with salt and freshly ground black pepper and mix well.
2 Melt half the butter in a shallow skillet and add the potato mixture. Flatten it down with a wooden spoon or spatula and cook over moderate heat for about 5 minutes until lightly browned.
3 Put a plate on top of the pan and turn the pan over so that the potato mixture falls onto the plate. Melt the remaining butter.
4 Slide the potato back into the pan so that the underside cooks. Cook for a further 5 minutes or so. Slide onto a warmed serving platter. Serve at once.

Baked potatoes with apple

SERVES 4

4 large potatoes, each weighing about ½ lb

½ medium tart apple

2 tablespoons butter or margarine

1 large onion, minced

4 sage leaves, chopped, or 1 teaspoon dried sage

½ teaspoon dry mustard

salt

margarine, for greasing

1 Preheat the oven to 400°F.
2 Scrub the potatoes and with a fork prick each one in 2 places on both sides. Bake the potatoes for 1½ hours.
3 Remove the potatoes from the oven (leaving the oven on), let cool slightly, then cut each one in half lengthwise. Scoop the cooked potato into a bowl, leaving the shells intact. Mash the potato well. Pare, core and finely chop the apple.
4 Melt the margarine in a small skillet, add the onion and sauté gently

Left: The potato cake, Rösti
Above: Creamy piquant cabbage

until it begins to soften, stirring occasionally. Stir in the apple and cook for 2-3 minutes, until soft.
5 Stir the apple and onion mixture into the mashed potato. Add the sage, mustard and a little salt. Mix well.
6 Spoon the mixture back into the potato shells and make criss-cross patterns on the top with a fork.
7 Put the potato shells in a greased shallow ovenproof dish and return to the oven. Bake for 15 minutes until the tops are browned. Serve the filled baked potatoes at once.

Creamy piquant cabbage

SERVES 4

1 head Savoy cabbage, weighing about 1¾ lb, quartered

salt

Sauce

¼ cup butter

½ cup all-purpose flour

2 cups vegetable stock

⅔ cup light cream

3 tablespoons medium-dry sherry

2 teaspoons Dijon mustard

2 tablespoons chopped fresh parsley

2 teaspoons lemon juice

freshly ground black pepper

1 Bring a pan of salted water to a boil, add the cabbage and bring back to a boil. Lower heat and simmer for about 10 minutes, until the cabbage is just tender.
2 Meanwhile, make the sauce: Melt the butter in a saucepan, sprinkle in the flour and stir over low heat for 1-2 minutes until straw-colored. Gradually stir in the stock, then simmer, stirring until thick and smooth.
3 Gradually stir in the cream, sherry, mustard and parsley and heat through gently. Remove from the heat and stir in the lemon juice and salt and pepper.
4 Drain the cabbage. Transfer to a warmed serving dish, pour over the sauce and serve at once.

Chinese-style leeks

SERVES 4-6

2 large leeks, cut in 2 inch lengths
2 tablespoons butter or margarine
1 onion, sliced
½ cup walnut pieces
4 celery stalks, chopped
4 cups sliced stem lettuce or
    celtuce, sliced
salt and freshly ground black pepper
few dashes of soy sauce

1   Melt the butter in a skillet, add the leeks and onion and sauté gently for 5 minutes until the onion is soft but not colored.
2   Add the walnuts, together with the celery, and sauté over moderate heat, stirring, for 3 minutes.
3   Stir the stem lettuce leaves into the pan and cook for 2 minutes more.
4   Season to taste with salt and pepper, stir in the soy sauce and cook for a further minute. Serve at once.

Baked red cabbage

SERVES 4

1 red cabbage, shredded
8 prunes
⅔ cup dry red wine
2 tablespoons butter or margarine
1 large onion, thinly sliced
1 large tart apple

1   Soak the prunes in the wine for 3 hours. Drain, reserving the wine. Halve and pit prunes.
2   Preheat the oven to 350°F.
3   Melt the butter in a Dutch oven. Add the onion and sauté gently until soft.
4   Meanwhile, pare, core and slice the apple, then add to the pot. Cook gently for about 5 minutes.
5   Stir in the cabbage and prunes. Pour in the reserved wine and bring to a boil. Cover the Dutch oven tightly, transfer to the oven and bake for 1 hour. Serve hot.

Below: A touch of the Orient with Chinese-style leeks
Right: Lemon gives Zesty carrots a deliciously tangy flavor

Zesty carrots

SERVES 4

4 cups thickly sliced carrots
finely grated rind and juice of 1 lemon
2 tablespoons butter
1 teaspoon light brown sugar
salt and freshly ground black pepper
⅓ cup water
lemon slices and finely chopped chives, for
  garnish

1 Put carrot slices into a saucepan with the lemon rind and the juice, the butter, sugar, salt and pepper to taste, and the water.
2 Place the pan over high heat and bring to a boil, then cover with a tight-fitting lid. Lower the heat and simmer gently for 40 minutes, until carrots are just tender and the liquid has reduced to a glaze.
3 Turn the glazed carrots into a warmed serving dish. Garnish with lemon slices and chopped chives.

Sweet and sour carrots

SERVES 4-6

2½ cups thickly sliced carrots
salt
2 tablespoons vegetable oil
1 onion, sliced
3 celery stalks, sliced
¼ cup blanched almonds, halved
Sauce
2 teaspoons soy sauce
2 teaspoons cornstarch
1 tablespoon brown sugar
1 tablespoon cider vinegar
2 teaspoons lemon juice

1 Cook the carrots in boiling salted water for about 10-20 minutes until barely tender – the carrots should be firm. Drain, reserving the stock.
2 Heat the oil in a skillet, add the onion and celery and sauté over moderate heat for about 5 minutes, stirring constantly. Make sure that the vegetables do not brown.
3 Add the drained carrots to the pan and stir to coat them in oil. Remove the pan from the heat.
4 Make the sauce: Mix together in a saucepan the soy sauce and cornstarch, then add the sugar, vinegar and lemon juice and stir in ⅔ cup of the reserved carrot stock.
5 Pour the sauce over the vegetables in the pan and bring to a boil, stirring all the time. Boil briskly for 3 minutes, stirring occasionally.
6 Turn the vegetables into a warmed serving dish and scatter with the almonds. Serve at once.

Stir-fried mushrooms with snow peas

SERVES 4

2 cups sliced button mushrooms

1/2 lb snow peas

salt

1 small sweet red pepper, seeded

1 tablespoon soy sauce

1 tablespoon dry sherry

1 teaspoon honey

1/4 cup sunflower oil

1 clove garlic, chopped

1/2 cup cashew nuts

1/4 cup water

1 Clean the snow peas, string if necessary and cut in 1 inch pieces. Blanch in a large pan of boiling, lightly salted water for 1½ minutes; drain, refresh in cold water and drain again.
2 Cut the pepper in matchstick strips. In a small bowl combine the soy sauce, sherry and honey.
3 Heat the oil and garlic in a wok or large skillet over a moderate heat.

When the garlic begins to sizzle, add the sliced mushrooms and strips of pepper and stir-fry for 2 minutes. Add the cashews and stir-fry for a further minute.
4 Add a good pinch of salt and the water and boil over high heat until the liquid has almost entirely evaporated. Stir the soy sauce mixture and pour into pan. Toss vegetables and nuts in the sauce, then add the snow peas. Stir-fry for 1 minute. Transfer to a heated dish and serve.

Peas and pears in tarragon

SERVES 4

1 package (10 oz) frozen peas

3/4 lb ripe, but firm pears

salt

2 tablespoons butter

1-2 teaspoons dried tarragon

freshly ground black pepper

sprigs of tarragon, for garnish

Above: Stir-fried mushrooms
Right: Peas and pears in tarragon

1 Bring a small quantity of salted water to a boil and cook the peas according to package directions.
2 Meanwhile, peel and core the pears and cut them in chunks. Melt the butter over very gentle heat, add the pears and sauté gently for about 5 minutes until soft but not mushy. Stir in the tarragon.
3 Drain the peas and add them to the pan, season to taste with pepper, then gently mix together, taking care not to break up the pears.
4 Turn the peas and pears into a warmed serving dish, scraping the pan to ensure the juices are added. Garnish with tarragon and serve.

● Tarragon has quite an unusual and distinctive aniseed flavor. If you are not familiar with the taste and are not sure how much to add, use just 1 teaspoon of dried tarragon the very first time you try making this dish.

Fried onion rings

SERVES 4

1 lb Bermuda onions
½ cup wholewheat flour
¼ teaspoon baking soda
large pinch of cream of tartar
large pinch of salt
1 egg
3 tablespoons milk
1 teaspoon melted butter
vegetable oil, for deep-frying

1 Make the batter: Sift together the flour, soda, cream of tartar and salt. Beat the egg and milk together, then stir in the melted butter. Add the flour mixture to the egg mixture and beat well until the batter is smooth and glossy. Set the batter aside while you prepare the onions.
2 Slice the onions in thin even rounds, then separate the rounds so that they fall into rings.
3 Preheat the oven to 225°F.
4 Heat the oil in a deep-fat fryer to 375°F or until a cube of stale bread turns golden brown in 50 seconds; it is important to have the oil just hot enough for frying, but not so hot that it burns the onions.
5 Scoop up several onion rings on the prongs of a large fork, dip them into the batter and allow the excess batter to drain back into the bowl. Drop the coated onion rings into the hot oil and fry for 3-4 minutes, until the batter is golden brown and puffed up.
6 Remove with a slotted spoon and drain on crumpled absorbent kitchen paper. Put them on a warmed dish, cover with foil and keep hot while you cook the remainder in the same way.

• If the onions should become slightly soggy while being kept warm drop them once more in the hot oil, just for a few seconds, then drain again and serve.
   A handy alternative way of slicing onions into rounds is to slice them before peeling. The skin easily slips off each round.

Creamed onions

SERVES 4-6

1½ lb onions
salt
⅔ cup sour cream
freshly ground black pepper
mild paprika
2 tablespoons butter or margarine
4 tablespoons day-old white bread crumbs
1 tablespoon chopped fresh parsley
2 hard-cooked eggs
parsley sprigs, for garnish

1 Cook the onions in boiling salted water for 15-20 minutes. Drain them thoroughly, reserving 1 tablespoon of the cooking liquid. Let the onions cool slightly, then pat them dry with absorbent kitchen paper.
2 Preheat the oven to 350°F.
3 Put the onions on a board and slice them. Arrange the sliced onions in an ovenproof dish.
4 Beat sour cream with reserved onion liquid and season with salt, pepper and mild paprika to taste. Pour the cream over the onions.
5 Melt the butter in a small skillet, add the bread crumbs and sauté for about 5 minutes over moderate heat, stirring frequently, until the crumbs are golden and crisp.
6 Remove the pan from the heat and stir in the parsley. Chop 1 hard-cooked egg and stir it into the sautéed crumb mixture. Spoon the mixture evenly over the onions.
7 Bake in the oven for 15 minutes. Meanwhile, slice the remaining hard-cooked egg.
8 Arrange the egg slices in a row along the top of the dish. Sprinkle with paprika, garnish with parsley and serve at once.

Mushrooms in vine leaves

SERVES 4

8 large flat mushrooms
12-18 vine leaves in brine, drained
¼ cup olive oil
2 teaspoons finely chopped fresh marjoram
salt and freshly ground black pepper

1 Preheat the oven to 350°F.
2 Rinse the vine leaves under cold running water, pat dry with absorbent kitchen paper, then lay half the vine leaves over the base of an ovenproof dish or roasting pan. Sprinkle 1 tablespoon of the oil over the vine leaves.
3 Leaving the mushrooms whole, lay them on top of the vine leaves, stem-side up. Sprinkle with the remaining oil and the marjoram, then season to taste with salt and pepper. Cover with the rest of the vine leaves.
4 Bake for 30-40 minutes.
5 Remove and discard the top layer of vine leaves, then divide the mushrooms and remaining leaves among 4 individual plates. Serve.

Turnip and potato toss

SERVES 4

¾ lb small turnips, cut in chunks
1 lb potatoes, cut in chunks
salt
2 tablespoons butter
freshly ground black pepper
2 tablespoons chopped chives

1 Bring the turnips to a boil in a large saucepan of salted water. Lower the heat and let simmer for 5 minutes. Add the potatoes, return to a boil, then lower heat again and simmer for a further 10-15 minutes until the vegetables are tender.
2 Drain the vegetables well and mash to a fine purée. Beat in the butter, then season to taste with salt and pepper. Alternatively, put the drained potatoes and turnips with the butter and seasoning into a blender and work until smooth.
3 Turn the puréed vegetables into a warmed serving dish and sprinkle with chopped chives. Serve at once.

Tomato braised celery

SERVES 4

1 lb tomatoes, peeled and sliced
2 large heads celery
salt
2 tablespoons butter or margarine
1 onion, chopped
freshly ground black pepper
2 tablespoons finely chopped fresh parsley
2 tablespoons sliced stuffed olives, for garnish
  (optional)
grated Parmesan cheese, to serve

1 Cut off the root end of the celery and discard it. Cut off the leaves and pull away the stringy, outer stalks. Wash the celery under cold, running water – brush the stalks with a small hard brush while washing them.
2 Cut the celery into 3 inch pieces. Bring a pan of salted water to a boil, add the celery, lower the heat and simmer gently for 3 minutes. Drain the celery thoroughly.
3 Melt the butter in a saucepan, add the onion and sauté gently for 3-4

minutes, until soft but not colored. Add the tomatoes, stir well and simmer for 3 minutes. Add the celery, season with salt and freshly ground black pepper to taste and stir in the chopped parsley. Cover the pan and continue to simmer for a further 10 minutes, or until the celery is tender.

4 Turn the vegetables into a warmed serving dish, garnish with the olives, if using, and serve at once with the Parmesan cheese.

Peppers in tomato juice

SERVES 4

1/2 lb green peppers, seeded and sliced
1/2 lb sweet red peppers, seeded and sliced
1 tablespoon vegetable oil
2 tablespoons butter or margarine
1 small onion, minced
1 clove garlic, minced (optional)
1 teaspoon dried rosemary
1/2 teaspoon sugar
11/4 cups tomato juice
salt and freshly ground black pepper

1 Heat the oil and butter in a skillet, add the onion and sauté gently for 5 minutes until soft and lightly colored. Add the peppers and garlic, if using, and sauté for a further 5 minutes.

2 Stir half the rosemary and the sugar into the tomato juice. Season with salt and pepper; pour into pan.

3 Simmer, uncovered, for about 10 minutes, stirring occasionally, until the peppers are tender and the tomato juice has reduced to a sauce. Transfer to a warmed dish, sprinkle with remaining rosemary and serve at once.

Baked parsnips with sour cream

SERVES 4

21/2 cups sliced parsnips
2 tablespoons vegetable oil
1 large onion, sliced
11/4 cups vegetable stock
1/2 teaspoon prepared English mustard
1/4 teaspoon mild paprika
2/3 cup sour cream

Left: Mushrooms in vine leaves
Above: Peppers in tomato juice

Topping

1 cup wholewheat bread crumbs
1/4 cup shredded Cheddar cheese

1 Preheat the oven to 400°F.

2 Heat the oil in a large skillet, add the onion and sauté gently for 5 minutes until soft and lightly colored. Add the parsnips and continue cooking gently for 3-4 minutes until the parsnips are pale gold and just beginning to soften.

3 Stir in the stock, mustard and paprika. Bring to a boil, then lower the heat slightly and simmer for 15 minutes. Remove from the heat and stir in the sour cream with a wooden spoon until it is thoroughly combined. Spoon the mixture into an ovenproof dish. Make topping: Mix the wholewheat bread crumbs with the cheese and sprinkle evenly over the top of the parsnip mixture.

5 Bake in the oven for 1 hour until crisp and golden on top. Serve at once, straight from the dish.

Curried spinach

SERVES 4

2 lb fresh spinach, stems and coarse midribs
    removed, or 1½ packages (10 oz size)
    frozen leaf spinach, thawed and drained

2 tablespoons vegetable oil

1 onion, chopped

1 large clove garlic, minced

1 teaspoon ground coriander

1 teaspoon ground cumin

½ teaspoon ground turmeric

¼ teaspoon ground ginger

¼ teaspoon chili powder

½ teaspoon salt

1 tablespoon lemon juice

1 Heat the oil in a large skillet, add the onion and garlic and sauté gently for 5 minutes until soft.

2 Add the coriander, cumin, tumeric, ginger, chili powder and salt and cook for 5 minutes, stirring constantly.

3 Shake the spinach well and add to the pan with only the water that still clings to the leaves. Add the lemon juice and cook for 10 minutes over moderate heat, turning the spinach until it softens.

4 Transfer to a warmed serving dish and serve the spicy curried spinach at once.

Okra Mediterranean-style

SERVES 4

1 lb okra, ends trimmed and blemishes
    removed

¼ cup vegetable oil

1 large onion, chopped

1 lb tomatoes, peeled and quartered

1 clove garlic, minced

1 teaspoon ground coriander

salt and freshly ground black pepper

coriander leaves, for garnish

1 Heat the oil in a large saucepan, add onion and sauté over moderate heat for 5 minutes.

2 Add the okra to the pan, stir to coat well with the oil, then add the tomatoes, garlic and coriander. Stir well to mix, then season to taste with salt and pepper.

3 Bring to a boil, then lower the heat slightly, cover and simmer for 30 minutes until okra is tender. Serve garnished with coriander.

Nutty zucchini

SERVES 4

1½ lb zucchini, cut in ¼ inch slices

2 tablespoons butter or margarine

2 cloves garlic, minced

¾ cup roughly chopped walnuts

generous pinch of salt

freshly ground black pepper

1 Melt the butter in a skillet, add the minced garlic and sauté gently for 1-2 minutes, until the garlic is soft and lightly colored.

2 Add the sliced zucchini, stir well to coat thoroughly in the butter, then sauté over low heat for 10 minutes, turning occasionally.

3 Add the chopped walnuts, the salt and a generous sprinkling of black pepper. Cook for a further 5 minutes until the zucchini are tender, stirring occasionally. Transfer to a warmed serving dish and serve at once.

Spicy red beans

SERVES 4

¾ cup red kidney beans, soaked overnight

2 tablespoons vegetable oil

2 onions, thinly sliced

1 clove garlic, chopped (optional)

½ teaspoon ground allspice

¼ teaspoon cayenne

2½ cups vegetable stock

2 tablespoons tomato paste

2 tablespoons distilled white vinegar

1 bay leaf

salt

1 Drain the soaked beans, rinse under cold running water, then place in a large saucepan and cover with fresh cold water. Bring to a boil, boil for 15 minutes, then drain the beans thoroughly.

2 Preheat the oven to 350°F.

3 Heat the oil in a Dutch oven, add the sliced onions, chopped garlic, if using, allspice and cayenne and cook over low heat for about 10 minutes until the onions are soft but not colored.

4 Stir the beans into the Dutch oven. Pour in the stock, increase the heat and bring to a boil. Add the tomato paste, vinegar, bay leaf and a pinch of salt. Stir to mix well.

5 Cover the pot and transfer to the oven. Cook for about 2 hours until the beans are soft and most of the stock is absorbed.

6 Discard the bay leaf, then taste and adjust seasoning. Serve the beans hot, straight from the pot.

Left: Curried spinach
Right: Nutty zucchini

Desserts

To complete a vegetarian meal, why not treat family and friends to a special dessert? Our selection includes appetizing creamy creations, as well as cool ices and fruit favorites.

Rich chocolate mousse

SERVES 6-8

2 squares (2 oz) dark German chocolate, broken in small pieces

3 tablespoons hot water

6 tablespoons superfine sugar

5 eggs, separated

1 cup unsalted cashew nuts, finely ground

1 1/4 cups heavy cream

pinch of salt

few whole cashew nuts, to decorate

1 Put the chocolate in the top of a double boiler or a bowl set over a saucepan of simmering water. Add the water and sugar and stir with a wooden spoon over low heat until the chocolate has completely melted and the sugar has fully dissolved.

2 Remove from the heat. Remove the top section of the double boiler or the bowl from the hot water. Using a balloon whip, beat in the egg yolks one at a time, beating well after each addition. Set the chocolate mixture aside to cool for about 15 minutes.

3 Lightly stir the ground cashew nuts into cooled chocolate mixture.

4 Put 1 cup of the cream and the egg whites in separate clean dry bowls. Whip the cream until standing in soft peaks. Beat the egg whites until standing in stiff peaks. Lightly fold first the cream, then the beaten egg whites into the chocolate mixture.

5 Pour the mixture into a glass serving bowl, cover with plastic wrap and refrigerate overnight or until set.

6 Just before serving, whip the remaining cream until standing in soft peaks. Pipe rosettes of cream around the edge of the mousse and top each rosette with a nut. Serve chilled.

Gooseberry fool

SERVES 6

1 lb green gooseberries

1/3 cup brown sugar

1/2 teaspoon ground cinnamon

pinch of ground cloves

1/4 cup water

1 1/4 cups heavy cream

mint leaves, to decorate

1 Prepare the gooseberries. Put them in a large saucepan with the sugar, spices and water. Cover and cook over a low heat for 20 minutes or until the fruit is very soft.

2 Put the cooked gooseberries into a bowl and break them up with a fork, but do not reduce them to a purée.

3 Whip the cream until standing in soft peaks, then gently fold into the gooseberries with a metal spoon.

4 Pile the fool into one large glass bowl or 6 individual bowls. Refrigerate for 1 hour, and decorate with mint leaves before serving.

Honeyed apricot whips

SERVES 4

2/3 cup dried apricots

1 1/4 cups hot water

2 tablespoons honey

1 1/4 cups plain yogurt

2 egg whites

2 ladyfingers or chocolate fingers, to serve

1 Put the dried apricots in a small bowl with the hot water and let soak for at least 4 hours or, if possible, overnight.

2 Turn the apricots and water into a heavy-bottomed saucepan. Add the honey, cover and simmer very gently for about 20 minutes, until the apricots are tender. Remove from the heat and let cool completely.

3 Purée the apricots with the cooking syrup and yogurt in a blender.

4 Beat the egg whites until they stand in soft peaks. Using a metal spoon, lightly stir 1 tablespoon of the beaten egg whites into the apricot purée mixture, then gently fold in the remainder.

5 Spoon the whip into stemmed glasses. Serve at once, or refrigerate until serving time. Serve with the cookies.

Sparkling syllabub

SERVES 2

1 thin strip lemon rind

2 tablespoons lemon juice

2 tablespoons brandy

2 tablespoons superfine sugar

1/4 cup sparkling dry white wine, chilled

3/4 cup heavy cream

1 Put the lemon rind, lemon juice, brandy and superfine sugar into a bowl. Cover and let stand for at least 3 hours.

2 Remove the lemon rind, pour in the wine and stir in the heavy cream.

3 Using a hand beater, beat the mixture until it is light and fluffy and will hold soft peaks. Divide the mixture equally between 2 large glasses, then refrigerate for 30-60 minutes. Serve chilled.

Rich chocolate mousse

Coeurs à la crème

SERVES 2

½ cup small curd cottage cheese
1 tablespoon superfine sugar
finely grated rind of ½ lemon
⅔ cup heavy cream
1 egg white
¾ pint fresh or frozen small strawberries or raspberries
extra superfine sugar, for sweetening

1 Line 2 heart-shaped *coeurs à la crème* molds with large squares of wet cheesecloth; this helps prevent the cheese mixture from sticking. Let the cheesecloth hang over the sides.
2 Pass the small curd cottage cheese through a nylon strainer into a bowl, add the superfine sugar and lemon rind and beat well until very soft.
3 Whip ¼ cup of the cream until it forms soft peaks, mix into the cheese mixture.
4 Beat the egg white in a clean, dry bowl until it stands in stiff peaks. Fold 1 tablespoon of the egg white into the cheese mixture to lighten it, then fold in the rest.
5 Spoon the cheese mixture into the prepared molds and smooth the tops. Fold the overhanging pieces of cheesecloth over the cheese mixture to enclose it completely. Put the molds on a flat plate and refrigerate them overnight.
6 About 1 hour before serving, sprinkle the strawberries with superfine sugar to sweeten.
7 To serve: Remove the molds from the refrigerator and unwrap the tops. Place a small serving platter on top of each mold, then carefully invert the plate and mold together. Shake gently, unmold, then carefully remove the cheesecloth.
8 Decorate with some of the fruit, then pour over the remaining unwhipped cream. Put the remaining fruit in empty molds and serve separately.

● Coeurs à la crème molds are heart-shaped with raised, perforated bases.

Rum and raisin cheesecake

SERVES 6

2 cups chocolate wafer crumbs
6 tablespoons melted butter
butter, for greasing
Filling
1½ cups cream cheese
2 tablespoons superfine sugar
2 eggs, beaten
1-2 tablespoons dark rum
3 tablespoons seedless raisins
Topping
1 teaspoon superfine sugar
⅔ cup sour cream
⅓ cup seedless raisins
¼ cup dark rum

1 Grease an 8 inch round springform pan.
2 Mix the wafer crumbs with the melted butter until evenly combined, then spoon into the greased pan and press evenly and firmly over the base. Refrigerate the crumb crust for 30 minutes.
3 Preheat the oven to 325°F.
4 Make the filling: Beat the cream cheese with a wooden spoon until creamy and smooth, then slowly beat in the superfine sugar and eggs. Add rum to taste, then stir in the raisins.
5 Pour the cheese mixture into the prepared pan and bake in the oven for about 40 minutes, until set. Turn off the oven heat and leave the cheesecake to cool in the oven, with the door ajar, for 1 hour.
6 Make the topping: Stir the superfine sugar into the sour cream, then spread the cream over the top of the cooled cheesecake, taking it almost to the edge. Cover and refrigerate for at least 2 hours. Meanwhile combine the raisins and rum and let soak until required.
7 To serve: Remove the side of the pan by placing the pan on an inverted pudding mold and easing the side down. Place the cheesecake on a serving platter and sprinkle the soaked raisins around the edge of the sour cream. Serve the rum and raisin cheesecake immediately.

Pashka

SERVES 16

3¼ lb cottage or small curd cottage
  cheese

1 cup chopped blanched almonds

⅔ cup candied mixed peel, chopped

1 cup seedless raisins, chopped

1½ cup candied cherries, chopped

1 cup plus 2 tablespoons butter, softened

3 eggs

1 cup superfine sugar, lightly packed

½ cup heavy or sour cream

1 teaspoon rose water

To decorate

blanched almonds

candied cherries

candied fruit

angelica

1 Put the cottage cheese in a cheese-cloth bag and hang over the sink for at least 12 hours to drain.

2 Rub the drained cheese through a strainer into a bowl. Mix the chopped almonds and candied peel, raisins and cherries with the softened butter, and mix into the cheese.

3 Beat the eggs with the sugar until they are pale yellow and frothy, then mix them into the cottage cheese mixture, beating thoroughly to eliminate lumps. Beat in the cream and rose water and continue to mix until completely smooth.

4 Line a new flowerpot, large enough to hold the dessert, with scalded cheesecloth, leaving plenty of material around the edge to fold over the top.

5 Pour the pashka mixture into the lined flowerpot, then fold the edges of the cloth neatly over the top of the pot.

Left: Creamy coeurs à la crème for that romantic occasion
Above: Rich and irresistible, Rum and raisin cheesecake

Place a small plate inside the pot and weight down.

6 Put the flowerpot on a wire rack in a shallow dish so as much liquid as possible drains from the pashka. Refrigerate for at least 12 hours.

7 Remove the weight and plate. To unmold: Invert a round platter on top of the flowerpot, then gently invert, holding pot and plate firmly. Carefully remove the flowerpot and peel away the cheesecloth.

8 Decorate the top and side of the pashka with almonds, cherries, candied fruit and angelica. Press gently but firmly into surface.

Pineapple cheesecake

SERVES 10

6 tablespoons butter, melted

2 cups zwieback crumbs

1 tablespoon grated lemon rind

1⅓ cups sugar

1 can (8 oz) crushed pineapple in syrup, well drained

3 cups small curd cottage cheese, strained

1 teaspoon salt

¼ cup all-purpose flour

3 tablespoons lemon juice

½ cup heavy cream

4 eggs

To decorate

⅔ cup heavy cream

canned pineapple chunks, halved

1 Preheat the oven to 325°F.

2 Make the crust: Stir the melted butter into the zwieback crumbs, then thoroughly mix in 1 teaspoon grated lemon rind and ¼ cup sugar. Reserve 4 tablespoons of the mixture and use the rest to line an 8 inch springform pan. Cover the crust with the crushed pineapple.

3 Put the small curd cottage cheese in a bowl and add the salt, flour, remaining lemon rind, lemon juice and cream. Beat the mixture thoroughly with a wooden spoon.

4 Beat the eggs with the remaining sugar until the mixture is light and fluffy. Fold the egg mixture lightly into the cheese mixture.

5 Pour the filling into the pan and sprinkle the top with the reserved crumb mixture.

6 Bake in the oven for 1 hour, then turn off the heat and let the cake stand in the oven for 1 hour. Transfer to a wire rack and let cool completely before removing the side of the pan.

7 To decorate: Whip the cream until standing in soft peaks, then pipe a cream shell border around the edge of the cheesecake. Spike the cream with pineapple chunk halves and serve at once.

Yorkshire curd tarts

MAKES 10

pie dough, made with 1 cup wholewheat flour (page 42)

Filling

2 tablespoons margarine

2 tablespoons superfine sugar

½ cup cottage cheese, strained

1 egg, beaten

grated rind and juice of ½ lemon

4 teaspoons half and half

⅓ cup dried currants

1 Preheat the oven to 400°F.

2 On a lightly floured surface, roll out the dough, then cut out as many rounds as possible using a 3 inch cutter. Knead the trimmings together, roll out and cut again to make 10 rounds altogether.

3 Line ten 2½ inch tart molds with the dough rounds. Refrigerate while you make the filling.

4 Beat the margarine with the sugar until pale and fluffy, then stir in the cheese. Add the egg, lemon rind and juice, half and half and currants and mix well.

5 Divide the filling equally among the dough-lined molds. Bake in the oven for 20-25 minutes, until the filling puffs up.

6 Let the tarts cool for 2-3 minutes, then remove from the molds with the aid of a small slim spatula. Leave on a wire rack to cool.

Cassata Siciliana

SERVES 8

1¾ cups Ricotta cheese

¾ cup superfine sugar

⅔ cup water

1 cup best-quality candied fruit

pinch of ground cinnamon

3 squares (3 oz) dark German chocolate, cut in small pieces

¼ cup pistachio nuts, blanched, peeled and chopped

½ cup Maraschino or another sweet liqueur such as Curaçao or Drambuie

1 lb sheet cake

Icing

4½ cups confectioners' sugar, sifted

7 tablespoons water

1 tablespoon lemon juice

1 Press the Ricotta cheese through a fine-mesh strainer and set aside. Pour the water into a heavy-bottomed saucepan and add the sugar. Heat gently until the sugar has dissolved. Bring to a boil, without stirring, and boil for 1 minute until a clear syrup is formed. Do not stir the syrup at all during boiling.

2 Meanwhile, cut ⅔ cup of the candied fruit into small pieces, reserving the best pieces for decorating the dessert.

3 Remove the syrup from heat, pour it over the Ricotta and stir vigorously until the mixture is glossy and smooth. Add the cinnamon, chocolate, chopped candied fruit, pistachios and half the liqueur and mix thoroughly.

4 Line an 8 inch deep round cake pan with waxed paper. Cut the sheet cake into thin slices and use about two-thirds to line the base and the side of the pan. Use the trimmings to fill in any gaps. Sprinkle over some of the liqueur to moisten the cake lining.

5 Spoon in the Ricotta mixture and cover it with a layer of sliced cake. Moisten the top layer with the remaining liqueur. Cover with plastic wrap and refrigerate for at least 3 hours or overnight.

6 Make the icing: Melt the confectioners' sugar with the water and the lemon juice in a heavy-bottomed saucepan over low heat until it evenly coats the back of a spoon.

7 Invert the cake onto a flat plate or cake board, pour the icing over the cake and let it run down the side. Smooth the icing neatly with a slim spatula.

8 Return the cake to the refrigerator for at least 5 minutes to allow the icing to set. Transfer the cake to a serving platter and decorate the center with the reserved candied fruit. Serve the cassata at once.

Fresh orange mold

SERVES 4

5 large oranges

¼ lb sugar cubes

1 cup water

2 teaspoons agar-agar

1 tablespoon Cointreau or Grand Marnier liqueur (optional)

fresh orange slices, to decorate

1 Chill a 3-cup metal mold in the refrigerator. Wash and dry the oranges. Rub the sugar cubes over the unpeeled oranges to extract the essence from the zest and place the sugar in a heavy-bottomed saucepan. Add half the water and stir over a low heat until the sugar is completely dissolved. Remove the sugar syrup from the heat and set aside until needed.

2 Squeeze the juice from the oranges, strain and measure out 1½ cups, making up this quantity with a little water if necessary. Combine the orange juice with the sugar syrup, then pour into a jelly bag or cheesecloth-lined strainer suspended over a clean bowl. Leave for about 30 minutes to drip through.

3 Sprinkle the agar-agar over the remaining water in a small pan and stir to mix well. Boil gently, until dissolved. Allow to cool slightly, then pour in a thin stream onto the strained orange juice, stirring constantly. Stir

Left: Cassata Siciliana makes a glamorous dinner party dessert
Above: Fresh orange mold tastes refreshing and looks stunning

in the liqueur if using.

4 Rinse out the chilled mold with cold water and pour in the strained orange mixture. Cover and refrigerate for about 8 hours or overnight, until the mold is set firm.

5 To unmold: Wring a cloth out in hot water and hold it around the mold for a few seconds, then invert a chilled, lightly moistened serving platter on top of the mold. Hold the platter and mold firmly and quickly invert them, giving a sharp jerk halfway over. When the mold and platter are completely inverted, give them a firm shake. Carefully unmold.

6 Arrange the orange slices around the base of the mold, in an overlapping pattern, just before serving.

cream until just thickened. Stir the frothy meringue mixture, then beat into the cream, about one-third at a time. Pour the syllabub over the crumbs and grapes, cover the glasses with plastic wrap and refrigerate for 1-2 hours, until the crumbs are moist and soft. Do not refrigerate for too long or liquid will collect in the bottom of the glass.

4 Just before serving, top each syllabub with slices of kiwi fruit. (If added too far in advance, the slices will lose their freshness.) Serve chilled.

Dried fruit salad

SERVES 6-8

2½ cups dried apricots (sharp rather than sweet)

1½ cups prunes

⅔ cup raisins or golden raisins

1 cup blanched almonds, halved

½ cup pistachios, halved, or pine nuts (pignoli)

¾ cup sugar

2 tablespoons rose water or orange-flavored extract

1 Put the dried apricots in a large bowl, together with the prunes, raisins, almonds, pistachios, sugar and rose water.

2 Pour in enough water to cover and leave for at least 48 hours, to let the fruit plump up and the flavors develop and blend.

3 Serve the salad with some of its syrup poured over the top.

Spiced pears

SERVES 6

6 firm pears

2 cups hard cider

¼ cup apricot jam, strained

¼ cup light brown sugar

¼ teaspoon ground cinnamon

2 whole cloves

thin strips of orange rind

juice of ½ lemon

1 Bring the cider, jam, sugar and spices slowly to a boil in a deep saucepan.

Grape syllabub

SERVES 6-8

1 lb grapes, halved with seeds removed

2 cups macaroons or amaretti cookie crumbs

2 large egg whites

½ cup superfine sugar

½ cup medium dry white wine

2 tablespoons brandy or sherry

1¼ cups heavy cream

2 kiwi fruits, peeled and sliced, to decorate

1 Divide half the grapes equally among 6-8 tall stemmed dessert glasses, then cover with half the macaroons. Place the rest of the grapes on top and finish with a layer of the remaining macaroons.

2 In a clean, dry, large bowl, beat the egg whites until standing in stiff peaks. Add half the sugar and beat until the meringue is stiff and glossy. Using a large metal spoon, fold in the remaining sugar. Gradually fold and stir in the wine and brandy.

3 In a separate large bowl, whip the

2 Peel the pears, leaving them whole and with the stems on. Immediately stand them upright in the saucepan, add the orange rind and lemon juice, cover tightly and simmer gently for 20-30 minutes or until just tender but not too soft.
3 Cut a thin slice from the bottom of each pear. Stand the pears upright in a serving dish. Boil the liquid in the uncovered saucepan for about 10 minutes to reduce by half. Strain and pour over the pears. Leave overnight in the refrigerator. About 1 hour before serving, baste the pears well with the syrup.

Peaches Gorgonzola

SERVES 4

5 fresh peaches, peeled
3 tablespoons brandy
¼ cup mashed Gorgonzola or Dolcelatte cheese, rind removed
2 tablespoons heavy cream
1 tablespoon confectioners' sugar

1 Halve and pit peaches. Put 8 peach halves in a bowl; sprinkle with 1 tablespoon brandy. Let stand for 1-2 hours.
2 Blend the remaining 2 peach halves with the cheese. Add the remaining brandy, cream and confectioners' sugar. Blend until smooth. Refrigerate for at least 1 hour.
3 Divide the peach halves among individual glasses and top with brandied cheese cream. Serve at once.

Peaches and raspberries in wine

SERVES 4-6

4-6 large peaches, or 8-10 small ones
¾ pint fresh raspberries
1 cup sugar
1¼ cups water
2 cloves
3 sticks cinnamon
2-3 strips thinly pared lemon rind
2-3 strips thinly pared orange rind
1¼ cups white wine
whipped cream, to serve

Left: Grape syllabub
Above: Peaches and raspberries in wine

1 Place the sugar in a wide saucepan with the water and stir over a gentle heat until the sugar has dissolved. Add the cloves, cinnamon sticks and strips of lemon and orange rind and bring to a boil. Carefully lower the peaches into the syrup, reduce the heat and simmer, uncovered, for 5 minutes.
2 Add the wine to the pan and continue to simmer for a further 5-10 minutes, until the peaches are soft but not mushy. Remove the pan from the heat and take out the peaches with a slotted spoon.
3 Carefully peel off the skins with your fingers, then arrange the whole peaches in a shallow glass serving dish. Scatter the raspberries around the whole peaches.
4 Return the pan of syrup to the heat and simmer until the liquid has reduced to 1¼ cups. Spoon the hot syrup over the fruit and let cool, then refrigerate until ready to serve.
5 Serve the dessert very cold, with whipped cream.

Greengage purée

SERVES 4

2 ¼ lb greengages, halved and pitted

¼ cup sugar

2 cups water

1 cinnamon stick (optional)

1 Put the sugar and water in a large heavy-bottomed saucepan. Heat gently until the sugar has dissolved, then add the cinnamon stick, if using. Bring slowly to a boil and boil rapidly for 2 minutes to make syrup.

2 Remove the pan from the heat and add the greengages, skin-side down. Return the pan to the heat and simmer the greengages for 15 minutes until they are soft and pulpy.

3 Lift out the greengages with a slotted spoon and work them through a nylon strainer. Cook, then chill the purée for at least 2 hours.

Date and walnut baked apples

SERVES 4

4 large tart apples, each weighing about 7 oz

6 tablespoons natural, unsweetened apple juice

Filling

⅓ cup pitted dates, coarsely chopped

1 tablespoon chopped walnuts

2 tablespoons brown sugar

½ teaspoon ground cinnamon

1 Preheat the oven to 350°F.

2 Using an apple corer or a small sharp knife, remove the core from each apple. Score the skin around the middle of each apple with a sharp knife.

3 Make the filling: Mix together the dates, walnuts, sugar and ground cinnamon in a bowl. Use to fill cavities, pressing down firmly with the back of a teaspoon.

4 Place in an ovenproof dish, then pour the unsweetened apple juice carefully around apples.

5 Bake in oven for 50-60 minutes, basting occasionally with the apple juice, until the apples are soft when pierced through the center with a sharp knife. Serve the date and walnut baked apples at once.

Spicy apple crunch

SERVES 4

1½ lb tart apples
1 tablespoon light brown sugar
1 teaspoon ground cinnamon
2 tablespoons water
margarine, for greasing

Topping

¾ cup porridge oats
⅓ cup light brown sugar
¼ cup wholewheat flour
¼ teaspoon salt
3 tablespoons margarine, melted

1 Preheat the oven to 375°F.
2 Grease a shallow 6-cup ovenproof dish thoroughly with margarine. Pare, quarter and core the apples, then slice them thinly. Mix the sugar with the cinnamon. Layer the apple slices in the dish, sprinkling the spiced sugar mixture in between. Sprinkle over the water.
3 Make the topping: Mix the oats, sugar, flour and salt in a bowl. Stir in the melted margarine with a knife until thoroughly mixed.
4 Sprinkle the topping evenly over the apples. Bake in the oven for 50-60 minutes, until the apples are very tender and the topping is crisp and brown.
5 Serve the dessert hot or warm, straight from the dish.

Apple layer dessert

SERVES 4

2 lb tart apples, sliced
½ cup superfine sugar
juice and finely grated rind of 1 large orange
2½ cups soft wholewheat bread crumbs
⅔ cup light brown sugar
1 teaspoon ground cinnamon
margarine, for greasing
whipped cream, to decorate

1 Preheat the oven to 400°F. Grease a baking sheet with margarine.
2 Put the apples into a saucepan with the sugar and the orange juice. Cook over gentle heat for about 10 minutes until the apples are soft, then remove from the heat and beat to a smooth purée. Let cool.
3 Meanwhile, mix together the bread crumbs and brown sugar and spread over the greased baking sheet. Heat through in the oven, for about 15 minutes, turning every 4-5 minutes, until the sugar has caramelized and the crumbs have turned dark brown. Let cool.
4 When the bread crumbs are cold, put them in a plastic bag and crush them to small crumbs using a rolling pin. Transfer to a large bowl and mix the grated orange rind and cinnamon with the crumbs.
5 To assemble: Divide half the apple purée among individual glass bowls, then divide half the crushed crumbs over the apple. Spoon the remaining apple on top and finish with the remaining crumbs.
6 Top each serving with a swirl of whipped cream and refrigerate until ready to serve.

Left: Date and walnut baked apples
Above: Spicy apple crunch

30 minutes.

7 Meanwhile chill 4 large wine glasses and dip the rims in superfine sugar. Spoon the sherbet straight into the prepared glasses, and top each one with a red currant leaf. Serve the sherbet at once.

Wholewheat vinegar pie

SERVES 6-8

1/4 cup wholewheat flour
1 teaspoon ground apple pie spice
pinch of salt
4 egg yolks
1 cup light brown sugar
7/8 cup sour cream
3 tablespoons cider vinegar
3 tablespoons butter, melted
1 1/4 cups golden raisins
2 egg whites
whipped cream, to serve

Wholewheat pastry

2 1/4 cups wholewheat flour
1 teaspoon salt
1/3 cup butter
1/3 cup margarine
1/4 cup ice water

1 Make the dough: Sift the flour and salt into a bowl. Add the margarine and cut in until the mixture resembles fine bread crumbs. Stir in enough ice water to bind the ingredients together, then wrap in plastic wrap and refrigerate for 15 minutes.

2 Preheat the oven to 450°F. Roll out the dough and use to line a 10 inch diameter pie pan.

3 Make the filling: Sift the flour with the apple pie spice and salt. Place the egg yolks and sugar in a bowl and beat with an electric beater for about 10 minutes, or until the mixture is pale and thick, and leaves a trail.

4 Stir in the flour mixture, sour cream, cider vinegar and the melted butter. Beat until smooth, then add the golden raisins.

5 Beat the egg whites until standing in stiff peaks and fold them in. Pour the mixture into the pie shell, making sure the golden raisins are evenly distributed.

6 Bake in the oven for 10 minutes, then lower the heat to 350°F and cook for a further 20 minutes, until the filling is firm and brown. Serve the pie warm with a bowl of whipped cream.

Red currant sherbet

SERVES 4

1 pint red currants
1/2 cup water
1/3 cup sugar
1/4 cup red wine
1 tablespoon confectioners' sugar, sifted
1 egg white

To finish

superfine sugar
red currants or mint leaves

1 Pour the water into a heavy-bottomed saucepan and add the sugar. Heat gently until the sugar has dissolved, then increase the heat and boil the syrup for 3 minutes. Cool and set aside.

2 Put the red currants in a large saucepan with the wine. Cover and cook gently over a low heat for 15 minutes or until the fruit is soft and very juicy.

3 Rub the red currants through a fine strainer into a bowl, making sure no seeds pass through with the juice. Stir the confectioners' sugar into the purée, then gently stir in the cool sugar syrup.

4 Pour the mixture into a freezer-proof container and freeze for about 1 hour until slushy.

5 Transfer the mixture to a large mixing bowl, and beat until it becomes light in color. In a clean, dry bowl, beat the egg white until standing in stiff peaks, then fold into the red currant mixture.

6 Pour the mixture back into the freezerproof container and freeze for a further 1 1/2 hours, until it is just firm. Beat again in the mixing bowl, then pour back into the container and cover with a lid or foil. Freeze for a further

Hazelnut and raspberry meringue

SERVES 4

1 cup hazelnuts, skinned and crushed
2/3 pint fresh raspberries, hulled
4 large egg whites
1 cup plus 2 tablespoons superfine sugar
1/2 teaspoon malt vinegar
1 teaspoon rose water
1 1/4 cups heavy cream
2 tablespoons Kirsch
margarine, for greasing
flour, for dusting

1 Preheat the oven to 375°F.

2 Grease and flour two 8 inch round layer cake pans. Line the base of each pan with a circle of non-stick parchment or foil.

3 Beat the egg whites in a clean, dry bowl until standing in stiff peaks. Gradually beat in 1 cup of the sugar, 1 tablespoon at a time, until meringue is very stiff. Beat in the vinegar and rose water.

4 Carefully fold the nuts into the meringue with a metal spoon, then divide the batter equally between the prepared pans and smooth the tops. Bake in the oven, just above and just below center until the meringues are lightly browned, changing them over halfway through baking.

5 Remove the meringues from the oven and immediately run a slim spatula around the sides to loosen them. Let cool for a few minutes, then carefully invert them onto a wire rack. Loosen the paper on the bottoms with a round-bladed knife, then turn the meringues the right side up and let cool completely.

6 Whip the cream with the Kirsch and remaining 2 tablespoons superfine sugar until thick, but not buttery.

7 Invert 1 meringue round onto a flat serving platter, then peel off the lining paper. Spread with about one-third of the cream, then neatly arrange the raspberries on top, reserving a few for decoration.

8 Peel the paper off the remaining meringue and place on top of the raspberries, flattest side up.

9 Cover the top and side completely with the remaining cream, swirling it attractively with a spatula. Decorate the top with the reserved raspberries, then refrigerate for up to 2 hours until ready to serve.

Hot lemon soufflé

Left: Wholewheat vinegar pie makes a wholesome family dessert
Above: When you want to impress, serve Hot lemon soufflé

SERVES 4

2 lemons
3 large eggs, separated
4 tablespoons confectioners' sugar
2 tablespoons all-purpose flour
1 cup milk
1 large egg white
pinch of salt
butter, for greasing
sugar, for dusting

1 Generously grease a 5-cup soufflé mold with butter, paying particular attention to the rim. Coat with sugar, tipping out any excess. Preheat the oven to 425°F.

2 Grate the rind from 1 lemon and squeeze both the lemons to give 1/4 cup lemon juice. Reserve.

3 Put the egg yolks in a heavy-bottomed saucepan and stir lightly with a wooden spoon to break them up. Sift in the confectioners' sugar and beat until smooth. Sift in the flour and blend lightly until the mixture is smooth and free of lumps.

4 Put the milk in another pan and heat almost to the boiling point. Pour onto the egg yolk mixture in a thin stream, beating constantly and quite vigorously.

5 Put the pan over a moderate heat and cook, stirring constantly, until the mixture thickens. Add the lemon rind and juice and cook for a further 1-2 minutes until thick again. Pour the custard into a mixing bowl.

6 In a clean, dry bowl, beat all 4 egg whites with the salt until standing in stiff peaks.

7 Add a little of the egg white mixture to the custard and mix lightly. Fold in the rest of the egg white until well blended, then pour into the prepared soufflé mold.

8 Bake in the oven for 12-15 minutes until well puffed and golden. Serve.

egg yolks, whipped heavy cream, crushed bread crumbs and strong black coffee.

5 Turn the mixture into a 5-cup freezerproof container and cover securely with foil. Freeze for 2 hours, stirring lightly every 30 minutes, then leave for a further 2 hours, or until firm.

6 Let the ice cream stand at room temperature for about 5 minutes, to soften slightly. Decorate with mint sprigs or coffee beans if liked, and serve.

Lemon granita

SERVES 4-6

juice of 6 lemons

2½ cups water

¾ cup sugar

lemon twists, to decorate

1 Put the water and sugar in a saucepan. Heat gently until the sugar has dissolved, then bring to a boil and boil for about 5 minutes, without stirring, until a thick syrup is formed.

2 Remove the syrup from the heat and set aside until completely cold.

3 Add the lemon juice to the cold syrup and pour into a loaf pan or ice block trays without the ice block divisions. Freeze in the freezer compartment of a refrigerator or in the freezer for about 1 hour.

4 Remove from the freezer and stir well with a metal spoon until evenly mixed.

5 Return to the freezer and freeze for a further 3 hours, stirring with a metal spoon once every 30 minutes during this time, to form an icy slush.

6 Spoon the granita into individual glass dishes, decorate with lemon twists and serve at once.

Melon glacé

SERVES 4

1 melon, weighing about 2 lb

½ cup water

¼ cup sugar

1 cup unsweetened white grape juice

2 tablespoons lemon juice

Brown bread ice cream

SERVES 4

1 cup soft wholewheat bread crumbs

2 tablespoons sugar

2 large eggs, separated

⅓ cup light brown sugar, sifted if at all lumpy

⅔ cup heavy cream, whipped to soft peaks

1 tablespoon strong black coffee or dark rum

mint sprigs or whole coffee beans to decorate (optional)

1 Preheat the broiler to high. Mix the bread crumbs and sugar together; spread over the base of a small baking sheet and toast under the broiler for about 5 minutes, turning occasionally, until golden and crunchy.

2 Turn the crunchy toasted crumbs onto a plate and let cool completely, then crush roughly with the back of a wooden spoon.

3 Beat the egg yolks with a fork until well blended, then set aside.

4 In a spotlessly clean and dry large bowl, beat egg whites until stiff. Beat in brown sugar, 1 tablespoon at a time. Using a large metal spoon, fold in the

1 Pour the water into a heavy-bottomed saucepan and add the sugar. Heat gently until all the sugar has dissolved. Bring to a boil, without stirring, and boil for 1 minute. Let the syrup cool completely.

2 Cut the melon in half; remove and discard the seeds and any membrane. Scoop out all the flesh, drain and purée in a blender.

3 Measure 2½ cups of the melon purée and place in a mixing bowl. Stir in the cold sugar syrup, grape juice and lemon juice. Spoon the mixture into a freezerproof container and cover with foil.

4 Freeze for 1-1½ hours until mushy around the edges. With a fork or wooden spoon, stir the mixture well. Cover and freeze for a further 1½-2 hours, stirring every 30 minutes. The ice is ready to serve when it has reached an evenly-granular slushy consistency.

5 To serve: Work the ice lightly with a fork then spoon into individual bowls set on ice.

Strawberry ice cream

SERVES 4

1 quart strawberries, hulled
2 tablespoons frozen concentrated orange juice
1 cup heavy cream
3 egg yolks
⅓ cup superfine sugar
small sweet cookies, to serve

1 Purée the strawberries in batches in a blender. Add the frozen orange juice to the strawberry purée and stir well to mix. Cover.

2 Pour the cream into a heavy-bottomed saucepan, bring almost to a boil, then remove from the heat and let cool.

3 Beat the egg yolks and sugar until pale and creamy, then slowly stir in the cooled cream. Strain the mixture into a heatproof bowl.

4 Set the bowl over a pan half full of gently simmering water – check that the bottom of the bowl does not touch the water. Cook, stirring constantly until the custard is thick enough to thinly coat the back of the spoon. Remove the bowl from the pan, cover the custard closely with plastic wrap

and let cool completely.

5 Stir the custard into the strawberry purée and pour the mixture into a freezerproof container. Cover and freeze for 1 hour, or until frozen about ½ inch around the sides.

6 Turn the mixture into a bowl and beat thoroughly to break up the ice crystals. Return to the container, cover and freeze for a further 1½-2 hours until firm.

7 Remove from the freezer and let soften for about 45 minutes in the refrigerator before serving.

8 To serve: Scoop ice cream into individual glass dishes with an ice cream scoop and serve with crisp cookies, if liked.

Yogurt vanilla freeze

SERVES 4

⅔ cup plain yogurt
2 eggs, separated
⅓ cup superfine sugar
⅔ cup sour cream
1 teaspoon vanilla

Left: Brown bread ice cream
Above: Strawberry ice cream

To serve

2-3 small oranges, peeled and cut in sections
2 kiwi fruit, peeled and sliced

1 Beat together the egg yolks and sugar until pale and light. Then stir in the yogurt, sour cream and vanilla and mix well.

2 Spoon the mixture into a freezer-proof rigid container and place in the freezer for about 1½ hours until frozen solid around the edges but only softly frozen in the center.

3 Beat the egg whites until they stand in soft peaks, then fold them gently but thoroughly into the frozen mixture. Cover and return to the freezer for about 3 hours or until the mixture is solid.

4 Transfer to the main part of the refrigerator for 1 hour before serving, to let the mixture soften slightly.

5 To serve: Scoop the vanilla freeze into the center of 4 chilled small bowls, and surround with the orange sections and kiwi slices.

Baked Fare

Who can resist the aroma of freshly baked bread or the
sight of a delectable sponge cake? Spoil yourself with
any of these sweet and savory baked goodies.

Bara brith

MAKES 2 × 2 LB LOAVES

1⅓ cups golden raisins
⅔ cup dried currants
⅔ cup seedless raisins
2⅔ cups light brown sugar
2½ cups warm strong tea, strained
1 egg, lightly beaten
6 cups self-rising flour
2 teaspoons ground apple pie spice
vegetable oil, for greasing
1 tablespoon honey, for glaze

1 Put the golden raisins, currants, raisins and sugar in a bowl. Pour in the tea and stir well. Cover with a clean dish towel and let stand for 6 hours or overnight.
2 Preheat the oven to 325°F.
3 Grease and line with waxed paper two 9 × 5 inch loaf pans. Grease the lining paper.
4 Stir the beaten egg well into the fruit and sugar mixture. Sift together the flour and spice, then stir into the mixture until thoroughly combined.
5 Divide the mixture equally between the prepared pans. Smooth the surface of each.
6 Bake the loaves in the oven for 1½ hours, then lower the heat to 275°F and bake for a further 1½ hours, until a warmed fine skewer inserted into the loaves comes out completely clean.
7 Leave the loaves for a few minutes until cool enough to handle, then invert turn them onto a wire rack. Turn the loaves the right way up.
8 Put the honey in a small saucepan and heat very gently. Brush the tops of the warm loaves with the hot honey, to glaze. Leave until completely cold before serving.

Marmalade cake

MAKES 8-10 SLICES

2¼ cups all-purpose flour
1 teaspoon baking powder
½ teaspoon salt
½ teaspoon ground ginger
⅔ cup superfine sugar
½ cup diced butter
generous ½ cup coarse cut orange marmalade
½ cup milk
vegetable oil, for greasing

1 Preheat the oven to 375°F. Lightly grease a loose-bottomed 7 inch square pan, line sides and base with waxed paper, then grease the paper.
2 Sift the flour with the baking powder, salt and ginger into a bowl. Stir in the sugar. Add the margarine and rub it in with your fingertips until the mixture resembles even-size bread crumbs, then make a well in the center of the mixture.
3 Add 1½ tablespoons marmalade and the milk and mix with a large metal spoon until thoroughly blended. Spoon the batter into the prepared pan and level the surface. Using a fork, gently spread the remaining marmalade over the top, to within ½ inch of sides.
4 Bake the cake in the oven for 50-60 minutes, or until a warmed fine skewer inserted into the center comes out clean. Cover the pan with waxed paper after 35 minutes baking to prevent the topping scorching.
5 Cool the cake for 5 minutes, then remove from the pan and carefully peel off the lining paper. Let cool completely on a wire rack. For a more mellow flavor, wrap in foil and store for 2-3 days before serving.

Banana teabread

MAKES 12 SLICES

2 cups self-rising flour
½ teaspoon ground apple pie spice
½ cup margarine
⅔ cup light brown sugar
2 eggs
1½ cups mashed soft bananas
1 tablespoon brown sugar
vegetable oil, for greasing

1 Preheat the oven to 350°F. Grease a 9 × 5 inch loaf pan, line the base with waxed paper, then grease the paper.
2 Sift the self-rising flour and apple pie spice into a bowl.
3 Beat the margarine and sugar until pale and fluffy, then beat in 1 egg. Add the remaining egg and 1 tablespoon of the flour mixture and beat vigorously until evenly blended; a little flour prevents the mixture curdling when the second egg is added. Beat in the mashed bananas until well incorporated.
4 Using a large metal spoon, fold in the remaining flour mixture. Spoon the batter into the prepared pan and level the surface, then sprinkle over the brown sugar.
5 Bake in the oven for 1-1¼ hours, or until firm to the touch.
6 Cool the teabread for 1 minute, then run a slim spatula around the sides to loosen it, remove from pan and peel off lining paper. Turn right way up and leave on a wire rack to cool completely before slicing. This teabread is moist enough to serve plain, but can be buttered, if liked.

Bara brith is good with cheese

Wholefood carrot cake

MAKES 12 SLICES

2½ cups wholewheat flour

1 tablespoon baking powder

2 teaspoons ground apple pie spice

1 cup chopped Brazil nuts

⅓ cup chopped pressed dates

1 cup brown sugar

½ cup sunflower oil

½ cup unsweetened apple juice

2 cups finely shredded carrots

sunflower oil, for greasing

To decorate

15 whole Brazil nuts

8 whole dried dates, halved and pitted

honey, for glaze

1 Preheat the oven to 350°F. Grease a deep 8 inch square cake pan. Line the sides and base with waxed paper, then thoroughly grease the paper.

2 Put the flour into a large bowl. Sift in the baking powder and spice and stir well to mix. Stir in the nuts and

Above: Spiced honey bars
Right: Cheese and walnut teabread

dates. Add the sugar, oil and apple juice and beat with a wooden spoon until blended. Stir in the carrots, mixing well.

3 Turn the batter into the prepared cake pan and level the surface. Arrange the Brazil nuts and halved dates in rows over the top.

4 Bake in the oven for about 1¼ hours, or until a warmed fine skewer inserted into the center of the cake comes out clean. (Cover with waxed paper after 30 minutes baking to prevent overbrowning.)

5 Cool cake for 15 minutes, then remove from pan and peel off lining paper. Place the cake, the right way up, on a large wire rack and brush top with honey. Let cool completely before cutting.

• For a change, substitute almonds and candied cherries for the Brazil nuts and dates.

Spiced honey bars

MAKES 16 BARS

1 cup self-rising flour

1 teaspoon ground cinnamon

1 teaspoon ground apple pie spice

1 teaspoon baking soda

1 cup wholewheat flour

⅔ cup honey

juice and grated rind of 1 small orange

½ cup vegetable oil

½ cup light brown sugar

2 eggs, well beaten

¼ cup slivered almonds

melted margarine or vegetable oil, for greasing

1 Preheat the oven to 350°F. Grease a 9 inch square cake pan, which is about 2 inches deep. Line the base with waxed paper and then grease the lining paper.

2 Sift the self-rising flour with the ground spices and soda into a large bowl. Stir in the wholewheat flour, then set aside.

3 Pour the honey into a large bowl. Measure the orange juice and make up to ⅔ cup with boiling water, then add to the honey and stir with a wooden spoon until mixed. Stir in the oil, brown sugar, beaten eggs and grated orange rind.

4 Pour the honey mixture onto the flour mixture and mix thoroughly to make a smooth batter. Pour the batter into the prepared pan and sprinkle the almonds over the top. Bake the cake in the oven for 50-55 minutes, until well risen and springy to the touch in the center. (Cover with waxed paper after 40 minutes baking to prevent over-browning.)

5 Cool the baked cake in the pan for 5 minutes, then run a slim spatula around the edge. Invert onto a wire rack and peel off the lining paper – take care when inverting and removing the lining paper as the cake is very soft and cracks easily. Turn the cake the right way up. Let cool completely, then cut in 16 bars. Serve immediately or store in an airtight tin.

Cheese and walnut teabread

MAKES 8-10 SLICES

2 cups wholewheat flour
2 teaspoons baking powder
1 teaspoon celery salt
½ teaspoon dry mustard
¼ cup diced butter
1 cup shredded Cheddar cheese
¼ cup chopped walnuts
⅔ cup milk
1 egg, beaten
vegetable oil, for greasing
butter, to serve

1 Preheat the oven to 350°F. Grease a 7 × 3 inch loaf pan, line the base with waxed paper and grease it also.

2 Mix together the flour, baking powder, celery salt and dry mustard. Add the butter and cut it in until the mixture resembles fine bread crumbs. Stir in the cheese and walnuts, then mix in the milk and egg to make a soft dough.

3 Put the dough into the prepared pan, level the surface and make a slight hollow in the center. Bake for 40-45 minutes until the top of the loaf is golden brown and a warmed fine skewer inserted in the center comes out completely clean.

4 Leave the loaf in the pan for a few minutes before turning it out onto a wire rack. Peel off the paper and leave right way up, to cool.

5 Serve the bread, thickly sliced and buttered.

5 Cool the cake for 30 minutes, then remove from the pan and peel off the lining paper. Stand the cake the right way up on a wire rack and leave until completely cold.

Apricot spice round

MAKES 8 SLICES

2 cups wholewheat flour

1 teaspoon baking soda

1 teaspoon apple pie spice

1/2 teaspoon ground ginger

1/2 teaspoon salt

1/4 cup diced butter

2/3 cup chopped dried apricots

2/3 cup plain yogurt

vegetable oil, for greasing

wholewheat flour, for dusting

butter, to serve

Topping

2 tablespoons milk

2 tablespoons brown sugar

1 Preheat the oven to 425°F. Grease and flour a baking sheet.

2 Sift the flour, soda, spices and salt into a bowl. Tip the bran remaining in the strainer into the bowl. Add the butter and cut in until the mixture resembles fine bread crumbs. Stir in the apricots. Add the yogurt and mix until the dough is firm, then knead lightly until smooth.

3 Shape the dough into a round about 9 inches across. Place on the baking sheet and mark into 8 wedges. Brush the top with the milk and sprinkle the sugar over.

4 Bake in the oven for 25 minutes. Transfer the round to a wire rack to cool slightly and serve warm with plenty of butter.

Lemon dairy sponge

MAKES 6-8 SLICES

3 large eggs

6 tablespoons superfine sugar

3/4 cup all-purpose flour

vegetable oil, for greasing

Filling and topping

2/3 cup heavy cream

1 tablespoon milk

5 tablespoons lemon cheese

Dundee cake

MAKES 10-12 SLICES

2 cups all-purpose flour

1/4 teaspoon salt

1/2 cup finely ground almonds

2/3 cup dried currants

2/3 cup golden raisins

2/3 cup seedless raisins

1/4 cup candied cherries, rinsed, dried and chopped

1/3 cup chopped mixed candied peel

1 cup butter, softened

1 1/3 cups light brown sugar

finely grated rind of 1 orange

finely grated rind of 1 lemon

4 eggs, lightly beaten

1 tablespoon sherry, brandy, orange juice or milk

1/3 cup whole blanched almonds

vegetable oil, for greasing

1 Preheat the oven to 300°F. Grease a deep 8 inch round cake pan, then line the base and side with a double thickness of waxed paper. Lightly grease the paper with oil.

2 Sift the flour and salt into a bowl and stir in the ground almonds. In a separate bowl, mix the dried fruits, cherries and peel. Set aside.

3 Beat the butter, sugar and grated orange and lemon rind until pale and fluffy. Beat in the eggs, a little at a time, then fold in the sifted flour alternately with the fruit mixture. Stir in the sherry.

4 Spoon the cake batter into the prepared pan, level the surface, then arrange the almonds on the top. Bake for about 3 hours until brown and firm to the touch. Cover the cake with waxed paper if it browns too fast but avoid opening the oven door for the first hour of cooking or the cake may sink.

1 Preheat the oven to 375°F. Lightly grease two 8 inch layer cake pans, line their bases with waxed paper, then lightly grease the lining paper with vegetable oil.

2 Put the eggs and sugar into a heatproof bowl. Set the bowl over a pan of gently simmering water – check that the bottom of the bowl does not touch the water. Using a rotary or hand-held electric beater, beat until the batter is thick enough to hold the trail of the beaters for 3 seconds when they are lifted.

3 Remove the bowl from the pan and beat for a few minutes more, until the batter is cool. Sift one-third of the flour over the mixture, then fold it in with a large metal spoon. Add the remaining flour in the same way, taking care not to overmix.

4 Divide the batter equally between the prepared pans and spread evenly by gently tilting the pans. Bake at once in the oven for 15 minutes, until the cakes are golden and springy to the touch.

5 Cool for 1-2 seconds, then invert the pans onto a wire rack. Peel off the lining paper and let the layers cool completely.

6 To serve: Whip the cream with the milk until standing in soft peaks. Place one cake layer on a serving platter and spread with half the lemon cheese, then with half the cream. Place the other layer on top.

7 Put the remaining cream into a pastry bag fitted with a small star tip. Spread the remaining lemon cheese over the top of the cake. Pipe a border of cream around the top edge of the cake, then pipe a lattice over the lemon cheese.

Gingerbread

MAKES 8-10 SLICES

2 cups all-purpose flour
large pinch of salt
1½ teaspoons baking powder
½ teaspoon baking soda
1 teaspoon ground ginger
½ teaspoon ground apple pie spice
⅔ cup light brown sugar
6 tablespoons margarine
¼ cup molasses
¼ cup light corn syrup
1 egg
½ cup milk
grated rind of 1 orange
melted butter, for greasing

1 Preheat the oven to 325°F. Lightly grease an 8 inch square cake pan. Line the sides and base with waxed paper, then grease the lining paper.

2 Sift the flour with the salt, baking powder, baking soda, ginger and apple pie spice into a bowl.

3 Put the sugar, margarine, molasses and syrup in a heavy-bottomed sauce-pan and stir over a low heat until the ingredients are melted and thoroughly blended. Remove from the heat and let cool slightly.

4 Beat the egg with the milk and pour onto the sifted flour mixture. Add the cooled melted molasses mixture and grated orange rind. Using a metal spoon, stir until thoroughly combined.

5 Pour the cake batter into the prepared pan. Bake for about 50 minutes, until the top of the gingerbread is firm to the touch.

6 Let the cake cool in the pan for 10 minutes before inverting onto a wire rack. Remove the lining paper and leave the cake to become quite cold. Wrap the cake in foil and store for 3 days before cutting.

Left: Dundee cake
Below: Lemon dairy sponge

Frosted walnut cake

MAKES 6-8 SLICES

1 cup self-rising flour

pinch of salt

1/2 cup butter or margarine

1/2 cup superfine sugar

2 eggs, beaten

1/2 cup finely chopped walnuts

melted margarine or vegetable oil, for greasing

8 walnut halves, to decorate

Meringue frosting

3/4 cup superfine sugar

pinch of salt

pinch of cream of tartar

2 tablespoons water

1 egg white

few drops of vanilla

1 Preheat the oven to 350°F. Grease two 8 inch layer cake pans. Line each base with waxed paper, then grease the lining paper.

2 Sift the flour and salt into a bowl and set aside. Beat the butter and sugar together until pale and fluffy, then beat in the eggs, a little at a time. Fold in the sifted flour and chopped walnuts.

3 Divide the batter equally between the prepared pans and level the surfaces. Bake the mixture in the oven, just above the center, for about 25 minutes, until golden and springy to the touch.

4 Leave in the pans for 3 minutes, then invert onto a wire rack and peel off the lining paper. Turn the cakes the right way up and leave to cool completely.

5 Make the meringue frosting: Place the sugar, salt, cream of tartar, water and egg white in a heatproof bowl and beat together with a hand-held electric beater for 30 seconds. Set the bowl over a pan of gently simmering water (check that the bottom of the bowl does not touch the water) and beat at high speed for 5-7 minutes, until the frosting stands in peaks when the beaters are lifted out of the mixture. Remove the bowl of frosting from the pan of water and beat in the vanilla.

6 Place 1 layer on a serving platter and spread with a little of the frosting. Put the remaining layer on top. Working quickly, pile the frosting on top of the cake and spread it over the top and sides with a spatula, then mark it into decorative swirls.

7 Before the frosting sets, gently press the walnut halves around the top edge of the cake. Leave the frosting to set before serving.

Chocolate almond gâteau

MAKES 10-12 SLICES

1 cup all-purpose flour

1/4 cup unsweetened cocoa

4 eggs

3/4 cup superfine sugar

vegetable oil, for greasing

Mocha filling

3/4 cup butter or margarine

2 2/3 cups confectioners' sugar

4 teaspoons unsweetened cocoa

4 teaspoons hot strong black coffee

1 teaspoon dark rum

To decorate

1/3 cup apricot jam

1 tablespoon water

3/4 cup slivered almonds

3 squares (3 oz) semisweet chocolate, coarsely grated

1 Preheat the oven to 375°F. Grease a deep 8 inch round cake pan, then line the base with waxed paper and grease the lining paper with vegetable oil.

2 Sift the flour and cocoa into a bowl and set it aside.

3 Put the eggs and sugar into a large heatproof bowl. Set the bowl over a saucepan half-full of gently simmering water – check that the bottom of the bowl does not touch the water. Using a rotary beater or hand-held electric beater, beat until the mixture is thick enough to hold the trail of the beaters for about 3 seconds.

4 Remove the bowl from the pan and beat the batter for a few minutes more until it is cool. Using a large metal spoon, fold in the sifted flour, one-third at a time.

5 Pour batter into the prepared pan and spread evenly by gently tilting the pan. Bake immediately in the oven for 35-45 minutes until the surface is golden in color and springy to the touch. Let stand in the pan for 1-2 seconds, then invert onto a wire rack.

Left: Serve Frosted walnut cake as a special treat at coffee time
Right: Raspberry cream cake makes a grand finale to a dinner party

Peel off the lining paper and let the cake cool.

6 Meanwhile, make the filling: Beat the butter until creamy, then gradually beat in the confectioners' sugar. Dissolve the unsweetened cocoa in the black coffee, then beat into the filling with the rum.

7 Heat the apricot jam with the water until runny, then pass through a strainer. Return to the pan and boil until it thickens to a coating consistency, then let it cool.

8 Using a long serrated knife, cut the cooled cake horizontally into three layers. Use half the filling to sandwich the layers together.

9 Brush the apricot jam around side of cake, then press almonds onto the side using a spatula. Transfer to a serving platter.

10 Put the remaining filling in a pastry bag fitted with a ½ inch star tip and pipe a border around the top edge. Sprinkle the grated chocolate over the top of the cake, inside the border of cream.

Raspberry cream cake

MAKES 6-8 SLICES

1 cup self-rising flour
1 teaspoon baking powder
½ cup soft margarine
½ cup superfine sugar
2 large eggs, beaten
1-2 drops vanilla
melted margarine, for greasing
confectioners' sugar, to dredge
Filling
⅔ cup heavy cream
1 cup raspberries, thawed if frozen
4-6 tablespoons raspberry jam

1 Preheat the oven to 325°F. Grease the bases of two 8 inch round layer cake pans and line them with waxed paper; grease the lining paper.

2 Sift the flour and baking powder into a large bowl. Add the soft margarine, superfine sugar, eggs and vanilla and beat vigorously for 2-3 minutes until blended.

3 Divide the batter equally between the prepared pans, level each surface and make a shallow hollow in the center. Bake in the oven for 25 minutes until just firm to the touch.

4 Let the cakes stand in the pans for a few minutes before inverting onto a rack (to prevent their delicate surfaces being marked place a dish towel on the wire rack before inverting). Peel off lining paper. Turn cakes the right way up, then let cool completely.

5 Make the filling: Whip the cream until stiff. Lightly crush the raspberries and fold them into the whipped cream.

6 Spread 1 layer with half the jam, then with the raspberry cream filling. Spread the underside of the other layer evenly with the remaining jam. Cut it into 6-8 wedges (cut a thin strip off the last wedge), then position these, jam-side down and slightly apart, on top of the filling. Sift confectioners' sugar thickly over the top and serve the cake immediately.

Crispy lemon slices

MAKES 16 SLICES

6 tablespoons butter or margarine
1/2 cup superfine sugar
grated rind of 1 lemon
2 eggs, separated
1 cup self-rising flour, sifted
2/3 cup plain yogurt
1/4 cup cut mixed candied peel
margarine, for greasing
Topping
1/2 cup superfine sugar
juice of 1 small lemon
To decorate
16 candied lemon slices
32 small diamonds of angelica

1 Preheat the oven to 350°F. Grease an 11 × 7 inch jelly roll pan with margarine.
2 Beat the butter, sugar and lemon rind together until pale and fluffy. Add the egg yolks, one at a time, beating very thoroughly after each addition.
3 Using a large metal spoon, fold in the sifted flour alternately with the plain yogurt. Fold in the peel.
4 Stiffly beat the egg whites and fold them into the cake batter, using a large, clean metal spoon to cut through the batter.
5 Turn the batter into the greased pan and spread it evenly. Bake in the oven for 15-20 minutes until the cake is a light golden color and just firm to the touch.
6 Meanwhile, make the topping: Mix together the superfine sugar and lemon juice in a bowl to make a thin paste.
7 Let the cake stand in the pan for a few seconds, then carefully invert it onto a wire rack and immediately spread the lemon paste over the surface. (The paste sinks in to make a crispy top.)
8 Leave the cake until quite cold before cutting into 16 rectangles.
9 Just before serving, decorate the slices: Arrange a candied lemon slice and 2 diamonds of angelica on top of each slice.

Above left: Crisp and buttery Shortbread is a Scottish favorite
Right: Almond-flavored Macaroons are popular and elegant cookies

Shortbread

MAKES 8 LARGE SLICES

1/2 cup butter at room temperature
6 tablespoons superfine sugar
1 3/4 cups all-purpose flour
1/3 cup rice flour
butter, for greasing
superfine sugar, to serve

1 Preheat the oven to 325°F. Lightly grease and flour a 12 × 8 inch jelly roll pan or a 10 inch flan pan with a loose bottom and fluted sides.
2 Beat the butter and sugar together until pale and fluffy. Sift both flours into the butter and sugar, then mix well to form a dough.
3 Press the dough evenly into the pan, levelling the surface, then prick the top of the shortbread all over. Bake in the oven for about 40 minutes, until golden brown.
4 Mark the shortbread into sections while hot, then leave it to cool in the pan before turning out.
5 Just before serving, sprinkle the shortbread with a little superfine sugar. Break into sections to serve.

Oatcakes

MAKES ABOUT 24

1 1/2 cups fine or medium oatmeal
1/2 teaspoon baking powder
1/2 teaspoon salt
2 tablespoons butter
3-4 tablespoons hot water
margarine, for greasing
fine or medium oatmeal, for sprinkling

1 Preheat the oven to 400°F. Grease a baking sheet with margarine.
2 Put the oatmeal into a bowl with the baking powder, salt and butter. Mix together lightly with a fork, then add enough hot water to make a dough.
3 Sprinkle some oatmeal on a board and turn the dough onto this, kneading lightly. Roll out to a thickness of 1/8 inch and cut into circles with a cookie cutter.
4 Transfer the oatcakes to the prepared baking sheet and bake for about 15 minutes, until firm.
5 Cool on the sheet for a few minutes, before transferring to a wire rack. Cool completely before serving.

Macaroons

MAKES 18

1½ cups finely ground almonds
¾ cup superfine sugar
few drops of almond extract
few drops of vanilla
2 small egg whites, lightly beaten
blanched almonds, to decorate
extra superfine sugar, for sprinkling

1 Preheat the oven to 350°F. Line 2 large baking sheets with rice paper.
2 Put the ground almonds and sugar into a bowl and mix together well with a wooden spoon. Add the flavorings, then gradually stir in just enough egg white to give a fairly stiff consistency.
3 Put the mixture into a pastry bag fitted with a ½ inch plain tip. Pipe nine 1½ inch rounds onto each prepared baking sheet. Space rounds well apart, and away from the edges of the baking sheets, to give plenty of room for spreading.
4 Place 1 almond in center of each round; sprinkle lightly with superfine sugar. Bake in the oven for 10-15 minutes, until just firm and beginning to color.

5 Cool the cookies for 1-2 minutes, then transfer to wire racks and let cool completely. Using your fingers, flake the excess rice paper off the bottom of the cookies. Serve at once, or store in a tin or other airtight container for up to 5 days.

High-fiber bread

MAKES 2 × 1 LB LOAVES

2 cups water
1 tablespoon light brown sugar
1 tablespoon active dry yeast
5 cups wholewheat flour
1 cup bran
2 teaspoons salt
1 tablespoon sunflower oil
1 tablespoon kibbled wheat
sunflower oil, for greasing

1 Grease two 7 × 3 inch loaf pans.
2 Put 1⅓ cups water into a small bowl and stir in ½ teaspoon sugar and the yeast. Let stand for about 10 minutes, or until frothy.
3 Put the flour, bran, salt and remaining sugar into a large bowl and stir. Make a well in the center of the dry ingredients and pour in the yeast mixture, the oil and ⅞ cup water. Mix to a dough, then turn out onto a lightly floured working surface and knead for 5 minutes.
4 Rinse out the mixing bowl, oil lightly and put in the dough. Cover with oiled plastic and leave in a warm place for 1 hour, until the dough has doubled in bulk.
5 Place the oven shelf in the center of the oven and preheat the oven to 450°F. Punch down the dough with your fist, then knead again for 1-2 minutes.
6 Divide the dough in half and shape each half into a loaf shape the length and width of the pans. Press the top of each loaf in kibbled wheat. Put the loaves into the pans, wheat side up, and press the dough well down in the corners.
7 Cover the loaves with oiled plastic and leave in a warm place for 20-30 minutes or until the dough has reached the top of pans.
8 Bake the loaves for 10 minutes, then lower the heat to 400°F and bake for a further 25 minutes, until the bread is crisp and brown and sounds hollow when removed from the pan and tapped on the base. Cool the loaves on a wire rack.

Rich corn bread

MAKES ABOUT 12 SLICES

1 cup cornmeal
1 cup self-rising flour
1 teaspoon baking soda
1/4 cup superfine sugar
2 eggs
2/3 cup milk
1/4 cup butter, melted
vegetable oil, for greasing

1 Preheat the oven to 400°F. Grease an 8 inch square baking pan.

2 Put the cornmeal in a large bowl, then sift the flour and baking soda on top. Add the superfine sugar and mix well.

3 Beat the eggs with the milk, then gradually stir into the flour mixture to make a smooth batter. Add the melted butter and mix again.

4 Pour the batter into the prepared pan and level the surface. Bake for 25 minutes, until risen and golden brown. Cool the bread in the pan, then cut in squares to serve.

Cottage loaves

MAKES 8

4 cups bread flour
1 teaspoon salt
1 teaspoon sugar
7/8 cup warm water
1 1/2 teaspoons active dry yeast
1/2 cup warm milk
1 medium egg, beaten, for glaze
vegetable oil, for greasing

1 Sift the flour and salt into a bowl.

2 Dissolve the sugar in a little of the water. Sprinkle in the yeast and stir the mixture until smooth, then add the remaining water. Leave in a warm place until bubbles appear on the surface (3-5 minutes).

3 Make a well in the center of the flour. Pour in the yeast mixture and the milk. Using a round-bladed knife, mix all the ingredients into a soft dough, adding a little extra warm water if necessary. Finish the mixing with your hands.

4 Knead the dough on a floured board for 5-10 minutes until it is smooth and not sticky. Return it to the bowl and cut a cross on the top.

5 Cover the dough with a damp dish towel or a sheet of greased plastic and leave in a warm place for 1 hour, or until doubled in bulk.

6 Preheat the oven to 400°F. Brush a large baking sheet with oil and dust it with flour.

7 Knead the dough again for 2-3 minutes. Divide the dough into 8 pieces. Cut each piece of dough into two unequal pieces. Shape into rounds. Place one small round on top of each large one. Push your finger through the center of both, making sure that a hollow remains.

8 Place the shaped loaves on the prepared baking sheet and cover them loosely with a damp dish towel or oiled plastic. Leave them in a warm place for 10-20 minutes, until they have risen by about one-third.

9 Brush the loaves with beaten egg, avoiding the baking sheet, otherwise the loaves will stick to it.

10 Bake the loaves in the oven for approximately 20 minutes or until they are golden and sound hollow when tapped on the base. Cool the cottage loaves on wire racks.

Wholewheat Chelsea buns

MAKES 8

1/2 cup milk

1 egg, beaten

2 cups wholewheat flour

1/2 teaspoon salt

2 tablespoons butter, diced

2 tablespoons light brown sugar

1/2 teaspoon ground apple pie spice

1/2 package (1/2 oz size) easy-blend active dry yeast

3/4 cup confectioners' sugar

vegetable oil, for greasing

Filling

1/2 cup dried currants

2 tablespoons cut mixed candied peel

1/3 cup light brown sugar

1/2 teaspoon ground apple pie spice

1/4 cup butter, melted

1 Heat the milk in a saucepan until warm, then beat in the egg and set aside until required. Grease an 8 inch layer cake pan.

2 Sift the flour and salt into a large bowl. Add the butter and cut in until the mixture resembles fine breadcrumbs. Stir in the brown sugar, spice and yeast, make a well in the center and pour in the milk mixture. Using a fork, mix to a soft dough.

3 Turn the dough out onto a lightly floured surface and knead for about 10 minutes, until smooth.

4 Shape the dough into a ball and place in a large oiled bowl. Cover with oiled plastic and leave to rise in a warm place for 1-1 1/2 hours or until doubled in bulk.

5 Meanwhile, make the filling: Mix the dried currants with the peel, sugar and spice, then stir in melted butter.

6 Turn out the risen dough onto a floured surface. Knead gently until the dough is back to original size, then roll into a 12 × 9 inch rectangle. Pour filling over the rectangle and spread to cover dough.

7 Starting at a short edge, roll up like a jelly roll, to enclose the filling. Brush the end with water and press to seal, then slice across into 8 pieces.

8 Place 1 piece, cut-side up, in the center of the prepared pan. Arrange the remaining pieces around it so that they are just touching. Cover with oiled plastic and leave in a warm place for 45 minutes or until risen.

9 Preheat the oven to 400°F.

10 Bake the buns in the oven for about 30 minutes until risen and golden brown. Transfer to a wire rack and let cool completely.

11 Make the icing: Sift the confectioners' sugar into a bowl, then stir in enough water to give a smooth coating consistency. Drizzle the icing over the top of the cooled buns before serving.

Flowerpot loaf

MAKES 8-10 SLICES

1 1/2 cups bread flour

1 1/2 cups whole wheat bread flour

1 teaspoon salt

1 tablespoon margarine

1 teaspoon easy-blend active dry yeast

7/8 cup hand-hot water

1 tablespoon bulgur

milk, for glaze

vegetable oil, for greasing

1 Season an unused, clean earthenware flowerpot measuring 5 1/2 inches across the top and 5 inches tall. To prevent the loaf from sticking, brush the inside of the pot very thoroughly with oil, then place the empty pot in a preheated 400°F oven for 15 minutes. Let the pot cool completely before using.

2 Mix the flours together in a large bowl with the salt. Cut in the margarine, then sprinkle in the yeast and stir well to mix. Pour in the water and mix to a firm dough.

3 Turn the dough out onto a floured surface and knead for 10 minutes, or until it is smooth and elastic, then shape it into a round.

4 Brush the inside of the seasoned pot very thoroughly with oil, then sprinkle in 2 teaspoons bulgur.

5 Place the dough in the prepared pot, pressing it down well. Cover with oiled plastic and leave in a warm place for about 1 1/4 hours, or until the dough has risen just above the flowerpot.

6 Preheat the oven to 450°F.

7 Uncover the dough and brush the top with milk. Sprinkle over the remaining bulgur and press it down lightly. Bake loaf in the oven for 30-35 minutes, until the top of the loaf is brown and crusty.

8 Cool the loaf for 2-3 minutes, then run a slim spatula around the side to loosen it. Remove the loaf from the pot, then place the right way up on a wire rack and let cool completely before cutting into slices.

● May also be baked as a cottage loaf.

Left: Cottage loaves
Below: Flowerpot loaf

Orange iced buns

MAKES 8

1 package (10 oz size) white bread mix

finely grated rind of 1 large orange

2 tablespoons superfine sugar

⁷⁄₈ cup hand-hot water

all-purpose flour, for dusting

vegetable oil, for greasing

To decorate

1-1¹⁄₃ cups confectioners' sugar

4¹⁄₂ teaspoons strained orange juice

few drops of orange food coloring

candied orange slices (optional)

1 Grease a large baking sheet with the vegetable oil.

2 Put the bread mix into a bowl, then stir in the orange rind and superfine sugar. Mix thoroughly. Add the water and mix well, first with a wooden spoon and then with your hand to make a firm dough.

3 Turn the dough out onto a lightly floured surface and knead for 5 minutes, then divide in 8 equal pieces. Shape each piece into a round, then roll each round to an oval, about 4 inches long.

4 Transfer the oval buns to the prepared sheet, spacing them well apart. Cover with oiled plastic and leave in a warm place for about 1 hour, or until the oval buns are risen and have doubled in bulk.

5 About 20 minutes before the buns are risen, preheat the oven to 425°F.

6 Uncover the buns and bake in the oven for 15 minutes, or until they are golden brown and sound hollow when tapped with your knuckles on the base. Transfer the buns to a wire rack and let cool completely.

7 Make the icing for decoration: Sift 1 cup confectioners' sugar into a bowl, then stir in the orange juice. The icing should be thick enough to coat the buns; if it is too runny, stir in a little more sifted confectioners' sugar. Tint the icing pale orange with food coloring.

8 Spread a little icing over the top of each bun. Decorate with candied orange slices, if liked, then leave the buns for about 30 minutes or until the orange icing is firm and set.

9 The buns are best served fresh on the day of making.

Luscious filled Devon biscuits

Devon biscuits

MAKES 7-8

2 cups all-purpose flour

1 teaspoon cream of tartar

¹⁄₂ teaspoon baking soda

¹⁄₂ teaspoon salt

¹⁄₄ cup butter, diced

¹⁄₂-²⁄₃ cup milk

vegetable oil, for greasing

all-purpose flour, for dusting

To serve

3-4 tablespoons strawberry jam

¹⁄₂ cup heavy cream, lightly whipped

1 Preheat the oven to 450°F. Grease a large baking sheet with vegetable oil and lightly dust it with flour.

2 Sift the flour with the cream of tartar, soda and salt, then sift again into a large bowl. Add the diced butter and cut it in until the mixture resembles fine breadcrumbs. Make a well in the center.

3 Pour in most of the milk and mix to a soft (but not sticky) dough with a fork, adding a little more of the milk if necessary. Gather the dough into a ball, turn it out onto a lightly floured surface and knead it lightly and briefly until smooth. The dough should be mixed quickly and handled as lightly as possible.

4 Either pat or lightly roll out the dough to a round about ¹⁄₂ inch thick. Using a 2¹⁄₂ inch round cookie cutter, cut out as many biscuits as possible. Lightly knead the trimmings together, pat or roll out again and cut out more biscuits.

5 Brush the tops of the biscuits with milk and place on the prepared baking sheet. Bake in the oven, just above the center, for about 15 minutes until risen and browned. Wrap the biscuits in a clean dish towel and let cool.

6 To serve, split each biscuit in half with your fingers; spread the bottom half with jam and the top with heavy cream, then lightly replace the top half.

● These biscuits do not keep well – serve them on the day of making.

Index